Visualization Power

How Scientists, Inventors, Businessmen, Athletes, Artists,
Healers and Yogis Can Improve Their Powers of Visualization and
Visual Thinking

BILL BODRI

Top Shape Publishing LLC
1135 Terminal Way Suite 209
Reno, NV 89502

ISBN: 0-9980764-3-0
ISBN-13: 978-0-9980764-3-0
Library of Congress Control Number: 2016917352

DEDICATION

To the scientists, mathematicians, inventors, innovators, artists, musicians, physicians, healers, entrepreneurs, businessmen, students, coaches, athletes and yogis who want to get better at what they do by improving their powers of visualization and visual thinking.

CONTENTS

ACKNOWLEDGMENTS

The inspiration for this book goes to Nikola Tesla, Napoleon Hill and the Yoga, Buddhist and Vajrayana visualization practices used for spiritual cultivation. These visualization exercises are designed so that you can quickly develop visualization talents not just for the world of mundane accomplishments, but also for healing purposes and for spiritual achievements if you so chose them.

My thanks goes to Steve Amarillo for creating the cover for this book, and for Marshall Adair for taking on the task of editing it, which I hope will lead people through to a greater mastery of visualization.

Our educational systems of today do not teach young children either advanced memorization or visualization techniques despite the fact that these skills are more useful than most of the academic subjects being taught. Therefore I also hope parents will introduce these lessons to their children so they can start using visualization abilities as quickly as possible. Furthermore, I hope this book finds its way to college students and athletes who are trying to master a chosen area of expertise. Visualization abilities can greatly benefit your life, and I hope to have presented enough examples of success as well as the easiest progression for developing them.

Chapter 1
INNOVATORS, INVENTORS AND SCIENTISTS

One of the most amazing inventors of all time was Nikola Tesla, who was a contemporary of Thomas Edison. Most people know about Edison - inventor of the phonograph and electric light bulb - but few know about Tesla and his accomplishments. This is unfortunate since the modern AC alternating current electrical system that we all have in our homes, electric motors, remote control and robotics were all invented by Nikola Tesla. Many people consider him a greater inventor than Edison!

Tesla is credited with nearly 300 amazing inventions worldwide, and many people have attributed his inventive abilities to the fact he had very strong powers of visualization.

From an early age Tesla started training his visualization powers. In his 1919 autobiography, *My Inventions*, he reported how he had strong imagination skills in his youth and experimented with various mental exercises to develop and control them.

"Every night (and sometimes during the day), when alone, I would start out on my journeys - see new places, cities and countries - live there, meet people and make friendships and acquaintances and, however unbelievable, it is a fact that they were just as dear to me as those in actual life and not a bit less intense in their manifestations.

"This I did constantly until I was about seventeen when my thoughts turned seriously to invention. Then I observed to my delight that I could visualize with the greatest facility. I needed no models, drawings or experiments. I could picture them all as real in my mind. Thus I have been led unconsciously to evolve what I consider a new method of materializing inventive concepts and ideas, which is radically opposite to the purely experimental and is in my opinion ever so much more expeditious and efficient."

In later years, Tesla was so accomplished in being able to create and manipulate pictures in his head that he could, with extreme precision, create complicated images of working inventions in his mind. He could visualize complicated machines with such extreme detail and accuracy that he could move directly to the stage of constructing them, without need of prototypes. Once built they worked exactly as intended.

In *My Inventions* he wrote, "I do not rush into actual work. When I get an idea I start at once building it up in my imagination. I change the construction, make improvements and operate the device in my mind. It is absolutely immaterial to me whether I run my turbine in thought or test it in my shop. I even note if it is out of balance. There is no difference whatever, the results are the same. In this way I am able to rapidly develop and perfect a conception without touching anything. When I have gone so far as to embody in the invention every possible improvement I can think of and see no fault anywhere, I put into concrete form this final product of my brain. Invariably my device works as I conceived that it should, and the experiment comes out exactly as I planned it. In twenty years there has not been a single exception. Why should it be otherwise? Engineering, electrical and mechanical, is positive in results. There is scarcely a subject that cannot be mathematically treated and the effects calculated or the results determined beforehand from the available theoretical and practical data. The carrying out into practice of a crude idea as is being generally done is, I hold, nothing but a waste of energy, money and time."

Tesla could not only develop and refine inventions in his mind, but could mentally use his visualization powers to take apart the proposed machine, fine tune it and even visually check it for wear and tear before ever actually turning it into a physical product.

Basically, his visual thinking powers made him a genius in the field of mechanical and electrical invention.

Tesla reported, "By that faculty of visualizing, which I learned in my boyish efforts to rid myself of annoying images, I have evolved what is, I believe, a new method of materializing inventive ideas and conceptions. It is a method which may be of great usefulness to any imaginative man, whether he is an inventor, businessman or artist.

"Some people, the moment they have a device to construct or any piece of work to perform, rush at it without adequate preparation, and immediately become engrossed in details, instead of the central idea. They may get results, but they sacrifice quality.

"Here in brief, is my own method: after experiencing a desire to invent a particular thing, I may go on for months or years with the idea in the back of my head. Whenever I feel like it, I roam around in my imagination and think about the problem without any deliberate concentration. This is a period of incubation.

"Then follows a period of direct effort. I choose carefully the possible solutions of the problem I am considering, and gradually center my mind on a narrowed field of investigation. Now, when I am deliberately thinking of the problem in its specific features, I may begin to feel that I am going to get the solution. And the wonderful thing is, that if I do feel this way, then I know I have really solved the problem and shall get what I am after.

"The feeling is as convincing to me as though I already had solved it. I have come to the conclusion that at this stage the actual solution is in my mind subconsciously though it may be a long time before I am aware of it consciously.

"Before I put a sketch on paper, the whole idea is worked out mentally. In my mind I change the construction, make improvements, and even operate the device. Without ever having drawn a sketch I can give the measurements of all parts to workmen, and when completed all these parts will fit, just as certainly as though I had made the actual drawings. It is immaterial to me whether I run my machine in my mind or test it in my shop.

"The inventions I have conceived in this way have always worked. In thirty years there has not been a single exception. My first electric motor, the vacuum tube wireless light, my turbine engine and many other devices have all been developed in exactly this way."

Temple Grandin

Dr. Temple Grandin, author of *Thinking in Pictures*, reports that she also had mental powers of visualization that were quite similar to Tesla's abilities. She wrote,

"I THINK IN PICTURES. Words are like a second language to me. I translate both spoken and written words into full-color movies, complete with sound, which run like a VCR tape in my head. When somebody speaks to me, his words are instantly translated into pictures. Language-based thinkers often find this phenomenon difficult to understand, but in my job as an equipment designer for the livestock industry, visual thinking is a tremendous advantage.

"Visual thinking has enabled me to build entire systems in my imagination. During my career I have designed all kinds of equipment, ranging from corrals for handling cattle on ranches to systems for handling cattle and hogs during veterinary procedures and slaughter. I have worked for many major livestock companies. In fact, one third of the cattle and hogs in the United States are handled in equipment I have designed. Some of the people I've worked for don't even know that their systems were designed by someone with autism. I value my ability to think visually, and I would never want to lose it. …

"Every design problem I've ever solved started with my ability to visualize and see the world in pictures. I started designing things as a child, when I was always experimenting with new kinds of kites and model airplanes. In elementary school I made a helicopter out of a broken balsa-wood airplane. When I wound up the propeller, the helicopter flew straight up about a hundred feet. I also made bird-shaped paper kites, which I flew behind my bike. The kites were cut out from a single sheet of heavy drawing paper and flown with thread. I experimented with different ways of bending the wings to increase flying performance. Bending the tips of the wings up made the kite fly higher. Thirty years later, this same design started appearing on commercial aircraft.

"Now, in my work, before I attempt any construction, I test-run the equipment in my imagination. I visualize my designs being used in every possible situation, with different sizes and breeds of cattle and in different weather conditions. Doing this enables me to correct mistakes prior to construction. Today, everyone is excited about the new virtual reality computer systems in which the user wears special goggles and is fully immersed in video game action. To me, these systems are like crude cartoons. My imagination works like the computer graphics programs that created the lifelike dinosaurs in Jurassic Park. When I do an equipment simulation in my imagination or work on an engineering problem, it is like seeing it on a videotape in my mind. I can view it from any angle, placing myself above or below the equipment and rotating it at the same time. I don't need a fancy graphics program that can produce three-dimensional design simulations. I can do it better and faster in my head.

"I create new images all the time by taking many little parts of images I have in the video library in my imagination and piecing them together. I have video memories of every item I've ever worked with -- steel gates, fences, latches, concrete walls, and so forth. To create new designs, I retrieve bits and pieces from my memory and combine them into a new whole. My design ability keeps improving as I add more visual images to my library. I add video-like images from either actual experiences or translations of written information into pictures. I can visualize the operation of such things as squeeze chutes, truck loading ramps, and all different types of livestock equipment. The more I actually work with cattle and operate equipment, the stronger my visual memories become."

William Dreyer

One of the major inventors in the early days of the biotech revolution was William J. Dreyer, Ph.D. who explained that he also shared some of Tesla's talents. When talking with Professor Jim Odds from the California

Institute of Technology, Dreyer explained, "When I'm inventing an instrument or whatever, I see it in my head and I rotate it and try it out and move the gears. If it doesn't work, I rebuild it in my head."

His report speaks to the same powers of visual manipulation that Tesla had. The common question we must ask is how did these men develop these amazing visual imagination skills? Before we answer, first let's consider some more individuals.

James Lovelock

The inventor James Lovelock, who also created the Gaia hypothesis, was also skilled at visual thinking and credited his success to visual imagination. He once said, "What I tend to do is wake up about five in the morning – this happens quite often – think about the invention, and then imagine it in my mind in 3D, as a kind of construct. Then I do experiments with the image … Sort of rotate it, and say, 'well what'll happen if one does this?' And by the time I get up for breakfast I can usually go to the bench and make a string and sealing wax model that works straight off, because I've done most of the experiments already."

Seymour Cray

Seymour Cray, the father of supercomputing, could also visualize an entire new computer in his head, build it and then have it perform exactly as he envisioned. He would often just visualize it and then build it without any intermediate steps. His skills were similar to those of Elmer Sperry, the inventor of gyroscopic stabilizers, who would simply design inventions in his head before putting them down on paper.

William Miller

Peter C. Patton, director of the Minnesota Supercomputer Institute, once compared Cray to William A. Miller, who designed the Offenhauser racing car. Patton said Miller "could design castings, have them made, machine them, assemble his engines, and expect them to work right the first time and produce the intended horsepower." After more than 40 years of team development efforts in internal combustion engine technology, Miller's engine "is still a standard, a mark to be beaten," he said.

Tesla, Grandin, Dreyer, Lovelock, Cray, Miller and even Walter Chrysler, who founded Chrysler Corporation, developed their inventions as mental images. What is common to all these inventors is that they could envision things within their own minds, rotate or manipulate the images in various ways, and examine them from every angle.

Few of us can match the intensity, precision and mastery for detail in this form of visual thinking. The powers of Dreyer, Lovelock, Tesla and others simply astounds most of us who hear of it. Many of us have trouble creating motionless pictures in the mind, let alone moving images that can be closely examined and manipulated.

Today our scientists and inventors are using computers and 3D graphics to perfect their design ideas before turning them into concrete objects, but there is still the problem of time and expense with this approach. As Tesla noted, "The moment one constructs a device to carry into practice a crude idea he finds himself unavoidably engrossed with the details and defects of the apparatus. As he goes on improving and reconstructing, his force of concentration diminishes and he loses sight of the great underlying principle. . . ."

Even with today's computer imaging tools, wouldn't it be better to have these tremendous powers of visual imagination available to your mind? Could those skills be developed?

Works like *Talent is Overrated* and *The Talent Code* make the point that physical and mental skills can be developed through special types of training, such as the daily practice of imagining everything you did during the day backwards in your mind from latest to earliest. All sorts of visualization practices are possible just as memory skills are possible to learn. Therefore the question becomes what type of training practices could bring them about?

What Type of Visual Thinker Are You?

Let's start with the fact that psychologists recognize there are three types of visual thinkers. You can use the following questions to determine which type you are. Here are the questions.

Draw a square in your mind. Now, how did you do it?

Did you have to first draw it on a piece of paper or some other surface?

Did you need to close your eyes to draw the mental square (because physical seeing interferes with your internal image-making capabilities)?

Can you visualize a square with your eyes open and can you superimpose it on whatever you see in the physical environment (which actually is also just a picture in your mind)?

The most powerful visualization thinkers are this last group and can often mentally make the square become larger or smaller, change colors, become a 3D object, or move it through space. They can also change their viewing perspective. They can even project mental images onto the perceived scenes around them.

KASINA PRACTICE FOR GETTING STARTED

How might you develop such skills like this, such as what Nikola Tesla had mastered?

Start simple. Ancient Buddhist teachings found in Buddhaghosa's *Visuddhimagga* ("Path of Purification") suggest that you start by learning how to visualize very simple colors and shapes. In fact, there are various objects you can use for concentration practice, which the *Visuddhimagga* calls kasinas.

There are many types of kasinas that you can practice holding in your mind, such as the feeling of boundless love, peace or compassion. The ones we are interested in are those which can be visual meditation objects. You should practice visualizing them until you can hold their image steady in your mind.

The purpose of visualizing a kasina and holding it in your mind is to develop your powers of concentration without grasping at actual "objects." You first learn how to independently form images in your mind after looking at an image in the real world, and then learn how to manipulate these mental images.

A kasina, or starter object for concentration practice, is meant to be gazed upon. After you see it, then you try to hold that image in your imagination, or create an entirely independent image in your imagination. If you lose the picture of the image, you should open your eyes again and stare at it until you feel you have the mental ability to independently imagine it again.

In the different kasinas described within the *Visuddhimagga*, some are based upon the five elements - Earth, Wind, Fire, Water and Space. The ancient text did not say so, but as taught by neuro-linguistic programming (NLP) you should try to feel the wetness of water in your body, the heat and burning sensation of fire, the grittiness or heaviness of earth, the windy nature of air in movement and the spacious feeling of space when you are trying to visualize these elements. In other words, you are supposed to evoke sensory feelings within your body, in order to move your energy, when doing these visualizations. For instance, when visualizing fire you try to excite, energize, stimulate or activate all the energy within your body and feel your body as if it is a/on fire.

Another set of kasinas for visualization practice include various colors, which Buddhaghosa taught you could visualize after staring at circles of earth made of those colors. In today's world, you could just use construction paper instead of piles of earth or clay. After seeing the color you try to imagine/visualize it in your mind, trying to hold the picture with stability for as long as possible. Colors have certain tested psychological connotations, but what you are after is a fluidity of visualization skills wherein you can visualize any color at all.

The *Visuddhimagga* only specified a few colors, but the idea is to build up visualization muscles for being able to visualize all the colors of the rainbow and later many objects in general. In getting started, you can restrict your efforts to just a few colors such as red, yellow, blue, green, black, white, copper (brown), silver and gold.

You should also try to learn how to visualize glowing light, or the shining nature of reflective light. This is important because many visualization methods for healing or spiritual practices will require you to be able to visualize colors inside your body with shining luminosity. This is because the more energizing the visualization, the more it will help you move your internal energy.

A common exercise is to practice visualizing a red triangle, blue circle, and yellow square. Mastering the basic shapes of triangles, circles and squares allows you to build up more complicated images.

Once you can visualize these simple shapes and colors, next try manipulating them by transforming their colors from one to another, making the images larger or smaller, rotating them, or changing your perspective of them. If you learn how to hold them steady in your mind then you can scan them from different angles, examine them in depth and rotate them any way you like, as could Tesla.

These exercises will get you started at visualization practice. They are the first step at mastering the power of visualization to change your life. To develop the visualization skills of a Tesla, you have to start by forming images in your mind and then later become able to move or manipulate them in various ways. With repeated practice you will get better and better at it, so by practicing this REGULARLY your visualization skills will improve bit by bit.

After mastering the circle, square and triangle you can move on to more complicated objects such as a rainbow, lightning, bell, net, golden sword or machete, guitar, tree, billiards on a pool table, sand in an hour glass dropping and filling the bottom, people, deities and so on. The more often you practice visualizations, the more you will build your visualization muscles and the easier it will be to visualize anything you want in your mind.

Leonardo da Vinci

When you look at the notebooks of Leonardo Da Vinci you will most certainly come to the conclusion that he had remarkable inventive and visual skills. When you look at his notebooks, such as the *Codex Atlanticus* or *Codex Madrid*, there are hundreds of drawings of ingenious machines and gear mechanisms with strange shapes and different numbers of teeth.

No one can say for sure whether da Vinci used visualization techniques, however he once wrote of a method similar to the Indian kasina meditation practice: "It is not to be despised, in my opinion, if, after gazing fixedly at the spot on the wall, the coals in the grate, the clouds, the flowing stream, if one remembers some of their aspects."

This is another standard visualization practice you should try: stare fixidly at an object, close your eyes, and then try to re-create the image in your mind. In the east people often stare at the geometric shapes of mandalas and yantras (spiritual geometric diagrams) to practice their visualization remembrance skills. This is a means of improving your focus and memory.

KINEMATICS

The notebooks of Leonardo, packed with diagrams of inventions, brings us to our third challenge, which is the world of kinematics.

The father of kinematics, Franz Reuleaux (1829–1905) was a German mechanical engineer of the late nineteenth century who became a lecturer at the Berlin Royal Technical Academy. His book, *The Kinematics of Machinery: Outlines of a Theory of Machines* was one of the very first complete presentations of the kinetic motion of machines (how they move because of the interworkings of component pieces) as an engineering subject. Reuleaux did an incredibly important service to humanity by designing a set of nearly 300 models of gears, crank mechanisms, linkages and other mechanical movements as a textbook supplement that were cast in iron and brass and sold to engineering schools throughout Europe and the United States.

Reuleaux's book, however, is far too complicated to use for beginner visualization lessons. A better one for this purpose would be Gardner Hiscox's *1800 Mechanical Movements, Devices and Appliances*. It provides numerous drawings of mechanical inventions you can use for visualization practice such as steam engines, valves, gears and other pieces of one-hundred year old technology. You can use it as an exercise book for learning how to mentally rotate an image or for visualization practice on how the various mechanisms interact with each other.

Henry Brown's *507 Mechanical Movements: Mechanisms and Devices* is the one I personally use to practice visualizing mechanical equipment in motion. It is a small book of 507 mechanisms along with a brief description of each item's usage and operation. Just figuring out how various gears should move, from looking at the pictures, is an exercise in itself. Luckily, the internet has videos available showing the movements of mechanisms that might stump you.

Some of the mechanisms in Brown's book are extremely simple and some are intricately complex, but overall they present a variety of the small components used in complex mechanical machinery along with how they move. These are the bits and pieces of equipment that engineers have had to become familiar with over the last few hundreds of years of development in order to build modern society.

Scientists, inventors, mathematicians, physicists, tinkerers, and anyone with an interest in developing mechanical visualization skills will find within this book a treasury of challenging visualizations to master. Christopher Polhem, who established a laboratory of machines in the 1700s to help Sweden's economic development, has suggested that the key inventions on history, since they serve as a sort of mechanical alphabet, are the lever, wedge, screw, pulley and winch. These five can serve as the focus of visualization practices.

VAJRAYANA

In the spiritual traditions of Tantric Yoga, Vajrayana Buddhism, Bön and Taoism (as well as in other traditions) the practitioners are often taught how to perform visualizations of sophisticated, complex mandalas, deities and palaces or heavens. These are the pictures you see in thankas, mandalas, religious paintings and yantra diagrams. You first concentrate on memorizing the images, and then learn how to evoke their memories or create new ones from scratch in your mind. In these traditions visualization practice is an exercise in focus and concentration and contributes to the cultivation of mental stability.

For these concentration practices, you train to hold a fully realized form in your mind without wavering. In other words, you concentrate on an image and then try to hold a stable picture of that image in your mind. This is the skill you must learn to master.

Two types of visualizations are normally practiced in these traditions.

The first is called "**front generation**." Front generation is a form of visualization practice in which the image (such as a mandala, geometric figure, spiritual deity, etc.) is visualized as being present in front of the practitioner - facing the practitioner. Sometimes this is described as "being in the sky before the practitioner." This is the less advanced form of visualization practice.

"**Self generation**" is the more advanced form of visualization practice. In self generation the image of a deity, power or spiritual force is created in the mind and then "merged with the practitioner" as an agent of self-transformation. The idea is to imagine that a force of great spiritual power (usually the image of a deity) *comes into your body* to energetically open up its Qi channels, which are its energy channels or acupuncture meridians. The practice is used to help people become more flexible (since it softens the body) and healthy. It also lays the foundation for later spiritual progress if the practitioner so desires and takes steps in that direction.

Most people are not ready for practicing the complicated images used in schools such as Vajrayana until they do a lot of preparatory visualization and other mental cultivation work. The visualization practices used in Vajrayana serve the multiple purposes of helping you develop stable concentration, empty your mind of random thoughts (because you learn mental focus), and develop visualization skills and visual thinking capabilities. Because the self generation type ultimately help transform the energy circuits of your body, they also help you become healthier and lay a foundation for advanced spiritual progress regardless of your spiritual tradition.

Chapter 2
MENTAL POWERS & MUSICIANS

Anyone can learn to develop extraordinary mental powers of visualization like Nikola Tesla. It just takes time and practice effort to build the skills. For instance, there is the amazing story of Mark Tew, blind since birth, who read a braille version of the book *Superlearning* in 1984.

Mark started practicing the accelerated learning techniques in *Superlearning* and soon his computer programming career took off. Although blind, due to his increasing skills he became the indispensible guy at his company for software troubleshooting. He was eventually promoted to be the chief debugger of all of his company's software programs.

Mark's story is recounted in the updated sequel *Superlearning 2000*, which says: "Using his new skills in relaxation training and visualization plus the slow Baroque music that facilitates a connection to the subconscious mind, [Mark] found it easy to mentally picture an entire computer program. He could remember it and see it in his mind. 'I can mentally find bugs because I can see what's happening with the program,' he says. He didn't even have to go through the braille printouts. He developed a talent for visualization like the great Nikola Tesla, who could run entire experiments in his mind."

The ability to visualize a computer program or even math equations in your head is a skill prized by many scientists, and especially mathematicians. Many scientists and mathematicians actually use visual thinking as their predominant mode of thinking in making scientific discoveries. Unfortunately, they had to learn these skills the hard way since there is no course on how to develop them. This is, in part, why I wrote this book.

Nobel prizewinning physicist **Richard Feynman** would often refer to how he used a graphical approach in his thinking, one such example being his invention of Feynman diagrams to help understand quantum mechanics.

He once said that he would visualize mathematical equations in his mind and in order to solve them would sometimes mentally put different colors on the superscripts of the equations. In interviews he also said he would visually see in his mind the character of the answer to problems and would try to develop a clear picture of the situation before turning to mathematics.

In Timothy Ferris's *The 4-Hour Chef*, Ferris recounts the story of a friend, Nakajima, who was able to correctly multiply 287 times 965 and then 156 times 643 in his head. The reason he could perform the feat is because he had used an abacus so extensively in primary school that he no longer needed it to compute. He simply visualized using the abacus, and in that way could make his calculations. This is a skill that anyone can develop with practice.

Many people can perform math through visual imagination like this. For instance **Flinders Petrie**, an eminent British Egyptologist, would work out sums by use of an imaginary slide rule in his head, visualizing only that part of it with which he was at the moment concerned. The lesson here is that engineers can therefore become better at their jobs, and achieve more significant things in their careers, if they learn how to develop their visualization skills.

Famous black hole physicist **Steven Hawkins**, paralyzed and wheelchair bound due to his affliction with amyotrophic lateral sclerosis, also admitted in an interview that "I tended to think in pictures and diagrams I could visualize in my head." For his most famous work on black holes, done with Roger Penrose, he would dictate equations to Penrose who would write them down. When working on his Ph.D. he had already proved that he could handle theoretic equations in his head.

Albert Einstein, Nobel prize winning physicist, is famous for his visual thought experiments. For instance, he once imagined that he was a passenger riding on a ray of light while holding a mirror at arm's length in front of him. Since the light beam he rode upon and the mirror were traveling at the same speed, and since the outstretched mirror was a little bit ahead of him in distance, no light could ever catch up to the mirror and reflect any image, so he would never see himself in the mirror. If scientists can learn to do thought experiments because they mastered the power of visualization, we would have many more Einsteins and breakthroughs in modern science.

Michael Faraday, one of the greatest electrical innovators of all time, lacked any mathematical education. Even so, despite what others would consider a great deficiency he originated the path breaking concept of electromagnetic fields by envisioning the stresses around magnets and electric currents as "lines of force" or "fields" in space. This visual conception of lines of force became a powerful way to think about electricity and magnetism. It took a while for it to catch on, but his visual way of thinking about things changed the world.

Without the help of a single mathematical formula, Faradays' visual imagination saw the entire universe populated by these curved tubes, or lines of force, which traversed all space. His idea was novel and revolutionary at the time, and eventually led to the invention of the first electromagnetic motor.

James Clerk Maxwell was also reported to be a visual thinker like Faraday, and would make a mental picture of every problem he considered. Both men would think in terms of pictures when making scientific discoveries. When Maxwell first heard of Faraday's lines of force as tubes in which electrostatic force flowed as in a hydrodynamic model, he later envisioned the force lines as parallel rotating cylinders separated by ball bearings rotating in opposite directions. Maxwell was a mathematician who greatly benefitted through visual thinking and was a proponent of visualizing things in order to understand them better.

For instance, after reading J. Willard Gibbs' works on how to represent the thermodynamics of fluids in a graphical fashion, Maxwell was so impressed with this visual approach that he used clay and plaster to sculpture 3D graphical models of his ideas. This was at a time (1874) when it was rare to use graphical tools to represent problems.

Jules Henri Poincaré, one of France's greatest mathematicians and theoretical physicists, was another great scientist who benefitted from mastering the powers of visualization.

Poincaré developed unique cognitive abilities in childhood including a visual or spatial memory that let him recall the page and line where he read something in a book. Gifted with poor eyesight, he could not see the chalk board clearly when studying higher mathematics so he also developed an auditory memory with which he could remember theorems by ear when most mathematicians would remember only by eye. This too is also a skill one can train to develop. Poincare would also use visualization to solve problems in his head and retained information in a pictorial way.

IMPRISONMENT, BLINDNESS & VISUAL IMAGINATION

Although locked inside his body with no hope of movement, Stephen Hawking has accomplished much in science due to his mental powers of concentration and visual thinking. In fact, many scientists and mathematicians consider it their predominant conceptual mode for making scientific discoveries. Internal visualization skills can actually *save your sanity* if like Hawkins, or those in prison or solitary confinement, you are somehow deprived of freedom. It can even be used by the blind.

English mathematician Nicholas Saunderson went blind after he was born, but became the Lucasian professor of mathematics at Cambridge

University, a position once held by Newton and now occupied by Hawking. "Imprisoned" by blindness, he still used his mind to make mathematical and even visual discoveries. Leonhard Euler, an 18th century Swiss mathematician, also made amazing mathematical discoveries through visual thinking while blind for the last 17 years of his life. Another blind mathematician, Bernard Morin, went on to become a master topologist, which is a mathematician who studies the intrinsic properties of geometric forms in space. Despite his blindness, he has earned renown for his visualization of an inside-out sphere, proving once again that to be more productive and creative in their careers mathematicians should consider undertaking exercises to improve their powers of visualization.

In the *Chicken Soup for the Soul* books by Jack Canfield and Mark Victor Hansen there is a story about **Major James Nesmeth**, who was a prisoner of war in North Vietnam for seven years. While imprisoned in the solitary confinement of his cage, he often experienced torture and deprivation. Nesmeth needed some way to occupy his mind and stay distracted from his daily discomfort so he turned to visual imagination.

Every day he would imagine that he was playing eighteen holes of golf on his favorite golf course, and in his visualization he imagined everything down to the last detail including the singing of birds, the smell of the grass, the weather, the clothes he was wearing, the grip of the club in his hands, and the arc of the ball after it was shot. After he was eventually rescued and returned home, it turned out that through visual thinking practice he had shaved twenty strokes off his average golf score when he played his first real game of golf since his imprisonment.

Interestingly enough, the Nobel laureate (for Medicine) **Francois Jacob** practiced in a similar way to Nesmeth. Every morning upon waking he began each day by mentally recreating his room, then his house, then his neighborhood and then the entire world whilst lying in his bed with his eyes shut.

Natan Sharansky, a computer specialist who spent nine years in a Siberian prison after being accused of spying for the U.S., decided that he would use his solitary confinement to train himself to be the world champion in chess. As a child he had been a chess prodigy and had learned how to play several games simultaneously in his head, which he had previously thought was a useless skill.

In his punishment cell there was no bed, table or chair (and certainly no chessboard with chess pieces) but while imprisoned Sharansky played himself in thousands of games of mental chess. After being released, he was able in 1996 to play and beat world champion chess player Garry Kasparov.

Chinese pianist **Liu Shikun**, who was imprisoned for seven years during China's Cultural Revolution, has a similar story to that of Natan Sharansky. After he was released from prison many people say he played better than ever. When people asked him how this was possible since they expected him to have lost his skills, he answered, "I did practice, every day. I rehearsed every piece I had ever played, note by note, in my mind."

MUSICAL PRACTICE

Liu Shikun's case brings attention to the fact that there is a large and growing body of evidence that mental practice, when done correctly, can make a difference in your playing of a musical instrument.

In one musical study, a group of participants mentally practiced playing a five-finger sequence on an imaginary piano for two hours a day while another group physically practiced the same passage on a live piano. The players who only practiced using their visual imagination skills ended up showing the same neurological brain changes as those who physically practiced for real, and they ended up showing the same reduction in playing mistakes!

The famous violin teacher **Leopold Auer** once told Nathan Milstein, one of the twentieth century's greatest violinists, "Practice with your fingers and you need all day. Practice with your mind and you will do as much in one and a half hours."

The legendary pianist **Arthur Rubinstein** followed this dictum because he would use his photographic memory to practice playing the piano mentally. En route to a concert, he would practice passages in his lap without the benefit of a piano. Vladimir Horowitz, his rival, is also said to have done an incredible amount of mental practice to reach his height of perfection.

Many musicians find that mentally practicing their performance – internally visualizing it and hearing it note by note - saves lots of practice time and improves their performance. Visualization skills, it seems, are something they should master.

As we will later discover in our investigation of sports visualization techniques, science suggests that mental practice activates the same neurons and regions in the brain as actual physical practice, which leads to the same changes in neural structure and synaptic connectivity. If so, mentally rehearsing music in your head can improve your music retention skills and your ability to perform it.

A study by Grace Rubin-Rabson in 1941 even proved this. Researching mental rehearsal and its effect on learning and memorizing piano music, Rubin-Rabson found that the intensive mental rehearsal of music saved the need for keyboard trials and was as effective for retention as a greater number of keyboard trials.

In other words, incorporating *mental rehearsal* into your physical practice sessions decreases the amount of physical practice needed to memorize a passage. Mental rehearsal (which involves visualizing your playing) will help you more quickly learn how to play an instrument!

You can call this "visualization practice" even though the primary modality is auditory imagination and kinesthetic imagination. To practice this way you should hear yourself inside your mind, imagine seeing and feeling your fingers play the notes, and experimenting to try out different changes as well as correct mistakes when relevant.

For musical visualization practice, you imagine what your instrument looks and feels like (which is called kinesthetic imagery rather than visual imagery) as you are playing it, and you imagine the sound you want to make (auditory imagery) from the effort. There is both imagery you can imagine, or just sounds you can imagine such as how you can play better or create a new song or composition.

In fact, the great composers Mozart, Schumann, Wagner and Brahms have all used auditory imagining to create their own compositions. Mozart heard entire compositions in his head before writing them down, and Tchaikovsky also heard symphonies in his head before he put them on paper. Schumann once stated that he saw the music he wrote as "pictures ... clothed in lovely melodies."

Of course, if you are a musician who wants to practice this way you should also spend time in *real practice* going over the musical abilities you practice in your mind. You must always link mental skills with physical skills just as with kasina visualization you link mental imaginations with sensations you try to evoke within your body.

These auditory skills are not "visualization" skills in the sense that they involve seeing, but like visualization, they are mental skills that can also be learned and developed so that you can become a more creative composer or simply play music better. Once again, this requires a practice method and then hard practice. When Tibetans set out to master mandala visualizations, for instance, many practice mentally generating millions over the course of their lives. This is why they develop excellent visualization skills which they use to project images into others when their spiritual cultivation reaches a certain stage of development.

This method can be applied by musical performers to help ease performance anxiety. To reduce performance anxiety you should visualize a musical performance exactly as it will happen including what you are wearing as you walk on stage, playing the piece perfectly without errors, hearing the audience's applause, bowing and leaving.

Chapter 3
FROM CONCENTRATION TO
VISUAL DREAM SOLUTIONS

Einstein, Maxwell, Feynman and Hawkins are some of the most famous scientists of all time. A common denominator in their careers is that all had developed tremendous powers of concentration and relied upon visual thinking for their problem solving.

Their great success and renown definitely demonstrates that scientists should be taught how to think in pictures to help solve problems, yet there are no courses for scientists on visualization exercises. Aspiring scientists should certainly spend some time in visualization exercises to increase their visual thinking skills and enhance their own careers. Visual imagery plays a great role in scientific creativity and scientific advance so it makes sense to pursue those skills.

In every college, university and even high school there should be visualization, concentration and memory skill courses because of the great benefits they offer.

Concentration is the key to success for all the different types of visualization practice because if you cannot ignore wandering, meandering thoughts you will never be able to form steady pictures in your mind that you can manipulate in various ways. Focus and concentration are mainstay skills of great scientists and thinkers, and yet our educational systems never teach people concentration skills so that they can develop stable minds.

We just expect individuals to already have these skills or learn them on their own and yet in our school systems we have children flit from subject to subject making it even more difficult for them to learn how to concentrate. Furthermore, we design curriculums in such a way that children now need to be entertained in order to learn. No one in life will be able to avoid facing adversity. Therefore what we need to teach children is how to focus and concentrate on problems, staying with them with grit, determination and perseverance, until they solve them. Visualization exercises are a way to teach such concentration.

Swami Vivekenanda once said, "The main difference between men and the animals is the difference in their power of concentration. All success in any line of work is the result of this. Everybody knows something about concentration. We see its results every day. High achievements in art, music, etc., are the results of concentration. An animal has very little power of concentration. Those who have trained animals find much difficulty in the fact that the animal is constantly forgetting what is told him. He cannot concentrate his mind long upon anything at a time. Herein is the difference between man and the animals – man has the greater power of concentration. The difference in their power of concentration also constitutes the difference between man and man. Compare the lowest with the highest man. The difference is in the degree of concentration. This is the only difference."

John Maynard Keynes once spoke of Sir Isaac Newton saying that concentration was his greatest skill: "Newton's great gift was the power of holding continuously in his mind a purely mental problem until he had seen straight through it … Anyone who has ever attempted pure scientific or philosophical thought knows how one can hold a problem momentarily in one's mind and apply all one's powers of concentration to piercing through it, and how it will dissolve and escape and you find what you are surveying is a blank. I believe that Newton could hold a problem in his mind for hours and days and weeks until it surrendered to him its secret."

Concentration skills, which you can learn through visualization practice, can make people great!

The public knows that concentration skills are so vital to problem solving that authors have immortalized this ability in books. For instance, at the beginning of every new case, the fictional Sherlock Holmes would sit back in his leather chair, close his eyes, put his long fingers together and sit in silence concentrating on the matter. He solved his cases because of being able to focus, concentrate and deduce proper conclusions.

Mental concentration is like using a lens to take the scattered rays of the sun and focus them into a bright beam that can produce intense heat and illumination. In ordinary affairs, when we focus all our energies on achieving a goal then all our actions, both voluntary and involuntary, will end up moving us towards its achievement. Similarly, when we focus our thoughts on problems, we will begin to solve them and create breakthroughs that move us ahead. As the great sage and political strategist Kuan Tzu once said, "You think, think, think deeply enough and the solution will arise."

Visual thinking is a particular type of concentration which is highly valuable for creative problem solving; visualization practice is a wonderful way to train your concentration skills. We should definitely be teaching concentration - and super memory - in our education systems.

TETRIS EFFECT

When you concentrate very deeply on a mental problem, and truly think, think, think about it, that mental effort can penetrate through to your subconscious mind. If your concentration is so deep that it *saturates* your conscious mind, then after a period of *incubation* your subconscious mind might even give you the solution to the problem through dreams. This is what is often called the "**Tetris Effect**."

Most people know of the addictive computer game Tetris (where at increasing speeds you strategically rotate, move and drop falling colored blocks onto a rectangular matrix) that was made available on video game consoles and home computers.

Due to its simple rules and highly addictive nature, people have been known to continuously play the game for hours. Some people play so much that they end up seeing images of falling Tetris shapes when they close their eyes or have dreams of falling Tetris shapes when sleeping.

This is the "Tetris Effect," namely that people devote so much attention to an activity that it begins to spontaneously show up in random mental images as well as dreams. When you concentrate on a problem very deeply, the same effect can happen in that it surfaces in your dreams, and in some cases what appears in your dreams will be a visual solution to your problem!

DREAM SOLUTIONS

Just as the Tetris Effect demonstrates, there is a remarkable history of scientists who pondered deeply over unsolvable problems, and who eventually found the solutions to those problems in their dreams.

Dmitri Mendeleev (1834-1907) is famous for having discovered the shape of chemistry's periodic table in this way. Mendeleev was obsessed with finding some way to organize the 65 chemical elements known at the time into some sort of organized fashion that explained their characteristics. The problem had consumed his attention for months without any breakthrough.

Mendeleev knew that the problem had to do with chemical weights, but couldn't find any solution to his problem. One day he wrote down the names of each element on a separate card along with its properties and atomic weight. He played with the cards, moving them about in many patterns for many hours without finding any solution until he finally fell asleep at his desk.

While sleeping he had a dream which contained the solution, and this is how the periodic table was formed. He later wrote, "In a dream I saw a table where all the elements fell into place as required. Awakening, I immediately wrote it down on a piece of paper." The arrangement pattern of the elements was so accurate that it even revealed elemental characteristics that had been incorrectly measured.

Louis Agassiz (18907-1873), who was at the time the world's foremost expert on fish species, had for weeks been unsuccessfully trying to comprehend the structure of a fossil fish in an obscure rock impression. Finally the solution came in a series of dreams over three nights.

He awoke one night convinced that he had seen all the missing features of the fish concealed in the rock, but when he tried to fix upon the image it escaped him. The next night he saw the fish again, but when he awoke his memory was blank again too.

He placed a pen and paper next to his bed before going to sleep on the third night, and towards the morning the structure of the fish appeared in his dream again. Half asleep and half awake, he copied down the imagery. Upon fully awakening in the morning, he was surprised to see in his sketches structural features that he thought impossible for the fossil to reveal. However, cutting away the stone under the guidance of his sketches he found it to be correct.

Niels Bohr (1885-1962), who some consider the father of quantum mechanics, had difficulties working out what the structure of an atom was. He had worked on many designs that didn't fit, until one day he dreamt that he was sitting on a sun composed of burning gas with all the planets hissing around on thin filaments. The sun, of course, was a symbol for the atom's nucleus while the planets were its electrons, and so from this dream was born the foundation for atomic physics.

In 1782, **William Watts** invented a new method for making lead shot for shotguns because of a dream. The standard process involved chopping metal into pieces and forming it into spheres as best as possible, which was not just time consuming and costly but produced an inferior product. One day Watt dreamt that he was walking through a heavy storm of tiny lead pellets instead of rain. When he awoke he interpreted the dream as meaning that molten lead, when falling through the air, would harden into small spheres and thus make the tiny pellets he wanted. When he tested the idea by building a shot-tower he found out that it worked.

August Kekule's (1829-1896) discovery of the structure of the benzene molecule in his dreams is world famous. The exact structure of the molecule had escaped him until one night in 1865 when he fell asleep in his chair after working on the problem, and began dreaming of atoms dancing. In the dance they gradually arranged themselves into the shape of a snake that turned around and bit its own tail. The snake in a loop continued dancing in his dream, and when he awoke he realized that the benzene molecules were made up of rings of carbon atoms.

This discovery, made possible by his dream, opened up an entirely new field of chemistry. In *Serendipity, Accidental Discoveries in Science*, Royston M. Roberts recorded Kekule's tale of how he made his discoveries: "I was returning by the last bus, riding outside as usual, through the deserted streets of the city. ... I fell into a reverie, and lo, the atoms were gamboling before my eyes. Whenever, hitherto, these diminutive beings had appeared to me, they had always been in motion. Now, however, I saw how, frequently, two smaller atoms united to form a pair; how a larger one embraced the two smaller ones; how still larger ones kept hold of three or even four of the smaller, whilst the whole kept whirling in a giddy dance. I saw how the larger ones formed a chain, dragging the smaller ones after them but only at the ends of the chains. ...The cry of the conductor, 'Clapham Road,' awakened me from my dreaming; but I spent a part of the night in putting on paper at least sketches of these dream forms."

Alfred Russell Wallace (1823-1913), who conceived the theory of evolution by natural selection, had traveled in South America and South East Asia observing and recording all the species he found trying to understand how the differences in species, due to geographic barriers, had come about. He had pondered the question for years but never found an answer. Finally in 1858 he had a vision due to hallucinations caused by a tropical fever. It was in those visual images that he found the theory of evolution by natural selection.

Another famous case of dreams providing a visual solution to a mental quest is **Elias Howe's** (1819-1867) invention of the sewing machine. His problem was trying to figure out where to place the eye of the sewing needle, which perplexed him tremendously.

His original approach was to follow the model of an ordinary needle and place the hole at the heel, or back end. However, that changed after he had a dream that he had to build a sewing machine for a king in a strange country.

Just as in real life, in the dream he could not figure out where to place the eye of the needle. He thought that the king gave him 24 hours in which to complete the machine and make it sew, and if he didn't finish then death was to be his punishment. He worked and worked but finally gave up and in the dream was being taken to be executed.

However, in the dream he saw that all the warriors were carrying spears that were pierced near the head, which was the answer to his searching. He awoke, jumped out of his bed, headed for his workshop and made a crude model of a working needle.

The fascinating case of the mathematician **Srinivasa Ramanujan**

(1887-1920), who had virtually no formal training in mathematics, also shows the power of dreams. Ramanujan made incredible mathematics contributions in the field of number theory and elliptic functions. He produced almost 4,000 proofs, equations and formulas in higher mathematics.

Ramanujan said that he arrived at many of his ideas from the images within his dreams. He said the Hindu Goddess of Namagiri[1] would appear in his dreams, show him mathematical proofs, and he would write them down when awake. Recalling one of his dreams he explained, "While asleep, I had an unusual experience. There was a red screen formed by flowing blood, as it were. I was observing it. Suddenly a hand began to write on the screen. I became all attention. That hand wrote a number of elliptic integrals."

Otto Loewi (1873-1961), the father of neuroscience, had the thought in 1903 that nerve signals were possibly transmitted using chemical instructions, but could not think of how to prove his conjecture. After pondering the problem for years, in 1920 he had a dream about a solution, woke excitedly during the night and scribbled down some notes about the dream. Like most of us, in the morning he could not remember his dream or read his notes but luckily he dreamed about the problem again.

In this dream he saw an experiment he could use to prove once and for all that the transmission of nerve impulses was chemical instead of electrical, and this time when he awoke he remembered it. He subsequently carried out research based on his dream and proved that signaling across neural synapses was based on chemicals (namely acetylcholine, which ironically is the neurotransmitter that promotes dreaming) as he had suspected so many years previously. In 1936 he won a Nobel Prize for his work, which ultimately was due to a dream.

Nobel laureate **Frederick Banting** (1891-1941) also owes his prize due to dreaming. He was strongly motivated to find a cure for diabetes because it had killed his mother. Searching for its cause, he had a dream to tie up the pancreas of a diabetic dog in order to stop the flow of nourishment, did so and discovered that this resulted in a disproportionate balance between insulin and sugar. Another dream led him to how he could develop insulin as a drug to treat the problem, and since then insulin has saved the lives of millions of people.

Even authors and musicians receive inspiration in dreams. **Robert Lewis Stevenson** dreamed the key scenes in *The Strange Case of Dr. Jekyll and Mr. Hyde*. **Paul McCartney** composed the entire melody for "Yesterday" in a dream he had in 1965. James Cameron reported that he

---

[1] Namagiri Thayar is a Hindu form of the Goddess Lakshmi worshipped in Namagiri, a town in Tamil Nadu, India.

received inspiration for the movie *Avatar* from a dream while Samuel Taylor Coleridge's poem *Kubla Khan* came to him in a dream. The poet John Keats, novelist Sir Walter Scott, poet Edgar Alan Poe, writer H. G. Wells and novelist J. B. Priestly have all reported that some of their work was inspired by dreams. Even the poet William Blake, who made his living as an engraver, said that a new method of copper engraving was provided to him in a dream.

CONCENTRATION & VISUALIZATION

These stories all show the ability of your mind to subconsciously solve problems by presenting solutions to your rational mind through pictures - *after* you engage in extensive concentration.

How does your mind arrive at such solutions? All we need to know is that concentration is the spark of ignition. You have to hold onto a problem continuously for a long period of time (cutting off distractions) and then sometimes your mind will solve the problem for you.

Visual thinking, the ability to think in images, can help you solve problems, but you should know that your subconscious mind will often present solutions to you in a visual fashion too.

Earl Woods, father of famed golfer Tiger Woods, is famous for how he trained his son to concentrate in order to play golf. He taught Tiger how to ignore mental distractions by persistently making noises (such as rattling the change in his pocket) or dropping a golf ball or by performing other distractions during Tiger's swing. The idea was to teach Tiger a champion's mentality - the mental aspect of the game - which is the skill of concentration. When Tiger was just a baby Earl would also sit him in a high chair to let him watch Earl hit balls into a net, which was like a visual movie being run over and over again to impress the movements of golf into his mind. This type of visual training is something that adult golfers employ by watching videos of perfect swings over and over again so that the perfect form sinks into their minds.

Concentration is the skill you need to develop for visual thinking and that concentration can in turn be strengthened by visualization practice. If you want to increase your powers of focus and concentration, there are few better ways than learning how to form stable visual images in your mind.

Concentration is a primary skill essential to most achievement in life, but our educational system is poorly structured for teaching children how to concentrate. Instructional classes are usually short, with children hopping from subject to subject to "keep up interest." However, from my own experience at the Taihu School in China (see *The Taihu School*) children attain superior results through lessons much longer than forty minutes in length and when a variety of subjects (arithmetic, health, science, etc.)

revolve around the same topic. You must reduce distractions and topic hopping so that children learn how to go deeply into topics and master the art of concentration. A topic or subject, which the children will usually forget, is not as important as mastering the skill of concentration they will use for life.

Concentration improves your ability to visualize images, which in turn improves your ability to visually solve problems in all sorts of fields. Becoming a better visual thinker requires many hours of concentration practice and one of the best methods of strengthening concentration is through visualization practice. In mastering how to hold a picture in your mind you will also learn how to ignore all thoughts in your head other than the visualization.

YOGA CONCENTRATION EXERCISES

There are many exercises from eastern spiritual traditions for teaching concentration, some of which I have detailed in my books *The Little Book of Meditation, Twenty-Five Doors to Meditation, Meditation Case Studies, Nyasa Yoga, Move Forward* and *Quick, Fast, Done*. Here are some specific visualization exercises from the Yoga tradition that can be used by anyone to improve concentration skills.

EXERCISE 1 – Visualize Solid Colors

One popular technique for developing concentration is to visualize a color in your mind and hold that image for as long as possible. Using the kasina visualization technique, you choose a color and then try to visualize a geometric shape filled in with that color such as a blue circle, yellow square or red triangle. Try to hold the picture steady in your mind and manipulate the 2D image if you can.

A more difficult exercise is to select a color, such as gold, silver or white, and imagine that absolutely everything in the universe is that color – you cannot see anything except that color because there are no phenomena other than that color. Therefore you *are that color* without a body. You are just a bodiless consciousness and all you see/experience is that color infinitely in all directions. Try to do that and remain in that state for as long as possible. For instance, imagine that you are a bodiless person inside a sun made of that color and all you see in every direction is just that color.

If you practice this long enough using bright, auspicious colors (white, silver, gold, etc.) rather than depressing colors it will also help move the energy within your body in a helpful way. The highest stage of this practice is to imagine that you are not a color but infinite empty space, boundless and bodiless, and all things appear within you though you lack a body.

EXERCISE 2 – Visualize Geometric Shapes

Chapter 1 described the visualization method of envisioning and then manipulating geometric shapes – circles, triangles, squares. This time, without first looking at a shape as done with the kasina visualization methods, you are to create a 2D shape in your mind and then turn it into a 3D shape such as turning a circle into a sphere, square into a cube or rectanguloid cuboid, triangle into a pyramid or cone, and so on. Use any color you like for this visualization exercise.

Next, mentally make the solid object larger or smaller, change its color and move it through space.

Next, try to project it in the real world such as by seeing in on a table top or in the air with your eyes open. This, in particular, is a useful skill to develop. You should practice projecting images in space and have them do whatever you want.

EXERCISE 3 – Visualize an Object

Sit still and focus on observing one object for one minute. Observe everything about it - its size, shape, color and any other details. When your mind wanders, bring it back to the object. Burn the image of the object it into your mind.

Now close your eyes and only think of that object. You will see in your mind that object. It may not be a perfect recreation of what you see in real life but try to visualize it anyway. When necessary, open your eyes to refresh your image and try again.

After starting this practice you will probably notice your mind wanders after a short period of time. If any other thoughts come into your mind during any type of visualization or concentration practice, simply bring back your focus of attention to the task at hand. Practicing in this way will increase your powers of concentration.

Later, without that object in front of you, the next higher stage of practice it to try to draw that image from memory. Try to remember what you saw with perfection.

EXERCISE 4 – Visual Images from Memory

For this exercise you pick an object you are familiar with and then try to visualize it in all its detail. You either bring up the image from memory or practice doing what you did in exercise 3.

The object could be a person, room or object. For instance, everyday you probably sit on a toilet in your bathroom looking at the same door and wall, but right now can you close your eyes and perfectly visualize what you usually see everyday? Can you right now visualize the face of someone you see everyday? Try doing this. It sounds easy but is difficult. This is an exercise in visual recall.

EXERCISE 5 – Counting Breaths

A famous exercise for improving concentration is to count the number of your breaths for a few minutes. You sit in a relaxed position, start counting your breaths from one to ten, and upon reaching ten you start again at one. Any time you lose your count due to straying thoughts you start at one again.

When distracting thoughts arise in your mind to interrupt your counting, you can either cut them off and go back to counting or simply acknowledge the thoughts and let then pass.

The more difficult but more advantageous practice proceeds further. It also involves your physiology (internal energy) so is profitable for both your visualization skills and for your health. Instead of counting breaths, you will breath in through one nostril (left or right) and try to feel that entire side of your body from head to toe while visualizing that it becomes a certain color (red, blue, yellow, gold, orange, white, green, blue, etc.). When trying to visualize that you change the color of your skin and flesh (alternatively you can just try to grab the sensation of feeling that half of your body) you should also try to feel the energy throughout every cell of that half of your body. Stay with that one breath (holding it) until you can do this or until you can hold your breath no longer, and then exhale.

Holding your breath sets a time limit for a segment of concentration practice, and the practice will also progressively alter your body's energy in a positive fashion if you continue doing it over time. There are benefits here for improving your health, improving your sports/athletic performance and for eventually attaining peak performance or flow states in general.

After you breath out, you breath in again through the other nostril and then try to feel the energy within the flesh of that entire half of your body. Once again, try to change its color while feeling all the energy and physical shape of that half of your body. Normally you visualize right side with the color red and the left side with the color blue. Try to grab that portion of your body through feeling. When you can do that then breathe out - or you can continue keep trying to do that while holding your breath until you can hold it no longer. Then breath out.

EXERCISE 6 – Dream More Often

It is hard to make yourself dream of something you want, but you can increase the frequency of your dreaming. To do this you need your Qi, or energy, to flood your brain before you fall asleep. Then your brain will use that extra energy to form dreams. To encourage this to happen you must take a deep breath (breath in deeply), and then *slowly* let the air escape out of your mouth with a "ssss" sound (the mouth is half closed) while letting an energy sensation flow up your neck into your brain/head.

This extra energy that enters your head, which Chinese call Qi, will over time open up the energy pathways into the brain (making thinking more efficient) and lead to more vivid dreaming states. Hence, if you are concentrating on a difficult problem and need a solution, try mastering this technique and see if it might help create a dream breakthrough.

It is a proven fact that "deep thinking," which means staying on a problem with concentration, can so affect your subconscious mind that it ends up producing visual solutions that can protrude through to your dreams.

You can also develop visual thinking skills to help you solve problems without depending on dreams but this requires visualization practice. The key to better visualization skills is concentration practice of all types.

The best concentration practices come from the east, such as from Yoga, and can involve concentrating on an object, on your breathing, on a mental image (visualization practice), on your body, or on your own thinking processes. Many items can be used as objects for concentration. The best ones don't just help you develop your visualization and concentration skills but also help you transform the energy of your body in a positive way.

An important benefit of concentration practices is learning how to ignore wandering thoughts so that you can develop a clear, steady mind. For instance, at one point in time in ancient China the Zen school relied heavily on the technique of having people concentrate on koans (sayings without meaning). The purpose was to tie up the omnipresent factors of thought and discrimination that are always operating in the mind. You cannot succeed at creating stable visualizations unless you can ignore wandering mental distractions. Visualization practice itself trains your concentration muscles to do this because you hold your focus and attention on an internal image rather than get distracted by random thoughts.

Visualization, which is the ability to form mental imagery as you want, is a mental skill that can be learned. It is a talent you can develop from scratch. It can be used to solve problems and can also serve as a tool for making your dreams and desires come true. What you concentrate on, through visualization, is also something you can work on to become real. As we will see, visualization can even affect your subconscious mind to help you change your habits and build success.

Chapter 4
VISUALIZATIONS FOR BUSINESS PURPOSES, GOAL SETTING AND PERSONAL DEVELOPMENT

We all have the power to master visual thinking and use it to help invent things or create solutions to problems. The concentration involved in visualization efforts also gives us the power to program our subconscious minds to find solutions to difficulties that sometimes appear to us in our dreams. We can also use visualization practice to help us attain excellence in performance skills such as playing an instrument, performing in athletics, speaking in public, or even making a sales call. Among other things, when you repeatedly imagine yourself doing exactly what you want in a perfect fashion without errors, you physiologically create the correct neural patterns in your brain for the envisioned performance level just as if you had physically performed the action.

Visually rehearsing an event in our minds creates neural patterns that teach our muscles (and emotions) to do exactly what we want them to do. The visualized patterns can stimulate the nervous system in exactly the same way that actual event practice does. Visualization efforts can therefore also help us train to have the capability *to access any emotions we want on call.*

Visualization exercises can therefore be used to help you develop positive qualities that you would like to cultivate in yourself such as self-confidence, patience, kindness, generosity, humor, courage or any other quality you'd like to embody. If you imagine seeing yourself as having those skills, and practice feeling the associated energy and emotional states involved with those skills, this practice over time will help you develop them.

For instance, you could consistently imagine what it would feel like and be like to embody a certain virtue and then try to hold that feeling for as long as possible. Eastern Yoga schools say that those feelings, held with intent for quite some time, will help open up your internal energy pathways connected with those virtues. This would make the cultivation of those characteristics much easier to attain as a permanent feature of your personality, and thus visualization rehearsals along these lines can help you with personal self-improvement efforts (which I have discussed in my book *Move Forward*). William James once said that the greatest discovery of any generation is that a human can alter his life by altering his attitude, and if you learn to master your emotions in this way then you will become able to change your life because you will learn how to shift your moods and emotions at will. Visualization practice is therefore an important tool you can use for personal development.

Visual thinking can certainly help us to create inventions, solve difficult math and scientific problems, and improve our sports, musical or other types of performances. Visualization practice can help us change our lives in a broader sense as well. Through visualization practice we not only can learn how to access emotions on cue, but can also slowly condition our subconscious mind to help us get what we want. For instance, by consistently visualizing yourself as attaining your goals in life (as a type of mental rehearsal) this can actually program you to work harder towards achieving them. Ultimately this will make them much more achievable. Putting this another way, just as planning and concentration skills help people attain their goals, visualization skills can also help you accomplish your goals too.

For ordinary situations that might require preparedness that you might improve through rehearsals – such as making a sales call, making a presentation, negotiating a deal, delivering a speech, asking for a raise, or attending a job interview – visualization practice can also be used to help you achieve better outcomes. Here is how this works.

When you use visual imagination and mental imagery to create visions of what you want in your life then you end up building an internal template of what you want to happen. These things won't just magically manifest because you strongly think about them or wish for them to occur. That's nonsense thinking. However, by relying on the mental patterns you visually build you can more easily – both consciously and subconsciously - start taking the steps that will make things happen in the direction you want. Due to performing mental rehearsals, you might quickly seize opportunities that you might normally let slip by and will certainly suffer less procrastination to handle a situation that you've mentally rehearsed handling.

Visualization practice can be a powerful, creative tool to help you achieve what you want in life. With just a little use of the power of your visual imagination you can assist yourself in making small shifts and changes that will improve your life.

Unbelievable? One proof of these claims is that weight loss efforts can be empowered when we visually imagine that we are the perfect person we want to be. A 2011 study published in the *Journal of Behavioral Medicine* found that people who used visualization imagery to see themselves *as the person they would like to become through exercise* actually burned more calories than those people who simply imagined themselves only working out or getting ready to do it. Visualization practice actually helped them achieve the reality they wanted.

In other words, if you imagine how trim, slim, good looking, and energetic you want to be then visualization practice, *together with actual efforts*, are a dual team that will help you to get there. Together with positive efforts, the visualization practice of building an internal template - imagining yourself to be a different you through mental images – will give you a better chance of becoming that way.

DOES THIS WORK?

Several famous people have applied this principle to their lives quite successfully, and their stories of grand achievement illustrate this approach.

For instance, movie star **Arnold Schwarzenegger** – bodybuilding champion, successful real estate investor and ex-governor of California – has used visualization practice extensively throughout his life. When preparing for bodybuilding contests (he won many world championships in this field) he would visualize his muscles getting bigger and developing the shape he wanted. He firmly believed that the visualization efforts in conjunction with his exercises would help him shape his muscles.

Schwarzenegger also used visualization to help mentally program himself for success. "It's all in the mind," he explained, "The mind is really so incredible. Before I won my first Mr. Universe title, I walked around the tournament like I owned it. I had won it so many times in my mind, the title was already mine. Then when I moved on to the movies I used the same technique. I visualized daily being a successful actor and earning big money."

Famous actor and comedian **Jim Carrey** also speaks about how visualization practice played a big role in creating his Hollywood career. When he was still a nobody he would drive himself to the top of the Hollywood Hills and sit in his car to do visualization practice. He would visualize, visualize, visualize and not let himself go home until he firmly believed the vivid pictures of success he was playing in his mind's eye and felt euphoria and elation from his efforts.

One of the legendary things Carrey did was write a $10 million check to himself for "acting services rendered" that he posted on his bathroom mirror so that he would see it everyday as a motivational type of mental programming. Several years earlier, when he was still relatively unknown, he had postdated that check for Thanksgiving 1995. The amazing coincidence is that just before Thanksgiving 1995 he actually signed a contract for the $10 million he had continually envisioned!

Best-selling *Chicken Soup for the Soul* author **Jack Canfield**, a proponent of peak-performance strategies, had never earned more than $8,000 in a year when he began the practice of daily visualizations in focusing on the goal of earning $100,000 in a year. After he started practicing, ideas began to surface in his mind after only a month of effort. When he began to program his mind through visualization, his brain finally found the solutions to his $100,000 objective and he achieved his goal in less than twelve months!

Recognizing the power of visualization to program his mind, when he was writing the very first *Chicken Soup for the Soul* book Canfield and his co-author decided to once again use it. They scanned a copy of the New York Times best seller list into their computer, typed *Chicken Soup for the Soul* into the number one position in the "Paperback Advice, How-To and Miscellaneous" category, and then printed several copies which they hung up around the office. In a story reminiscent of Jim Carrey's, in less than twenty-four months *Chicken Soup for the Soul* was actually the number one book in that category!

Famous marketer **Dan Kennedy**, re-publisher of *Psycho-Cybernetics* and a proponent of mental training, would often tell stories in his books and seminars about how he used the mental powers of visualization, affirmation and other methods to reprogram his mind for wealth.

Best-selling author and relationship expert **Dr. John Gray** also reports that he regularly visualized his tremendous national success for years before he finally achieved it. Even though he was presenting seminars for just fifty to seventy people, he would nonetheless regularly visualize speaking in front of thousands of people, which was a reality that eventually happened.

A personal friend of mine, who at one time had become the youngest Vice-president of the RCA Corporation, once told me that he would spend time accessing his internal energy while visualizing that he had tremendous confidence. Then he would practice energetically projecting authority energy into the room around him. At first he practiced being confident and projecting this type of energy to fill his study. Once he mastered this level of projection, he started practicing in an auditorium until he felt he could entirely fill that larger room with his aura of authority and confidence. Eventually he ended up going to an empty sports stadium where he regularly practiced projecting the energy of courageous confidence until he felt that he had mastered the ability to even fill the large stadium with this

Qi.

Despite his young age, he became so good at projecting authority energy due to his visualization practice and energy work that he could sit in a room of Navy admirals and grab the lead from even the Chief of Staff whom everyone was programmed to recognize as the main authority.

ACADEMIC STUDIES

One problem with these stories, as inspiring as they are, is that they are cherry-picked because a selection bias overlooks countless other people who also worked extremely hard taking all the rights steps to accomplish their goals (including doing the relevant visualization practices that might help) but who did not achieve them. We are just focusing on the winners who happened to use this tool while ignoring those who used it without achieving their objectives. As an aside, in *Quick, Fast, Done* you can learn about the 8M method for successfully achieving goals which you should use when the other methods of accomplishment might fail.

Another problem with these stories is that in reading them you might infer that visualization directly achieves outcomes whereas its major benefit is actually in helping you *master the process* that produces that outcome. In other words, these stories don't separate visualization's effect on successful Processes versus Outcomes.

You might mentally imagine achieving a successful Outcome all you want, but you still have to create an effective Process that is a means for getting there. Visualization helps you create and perform a mental dry run a chosen Process, and this preparation helps pave the way for successful Outcome. If you practice visualization on a regular basis, this motivation will also help you maintain the perseverance necessary for achievement as well.

It is certainly true that visualizing success can condition your mind to accept and even expect that outcome, which does have great benefits, *but it cannot guarantee that outcome*. Nonetheless, if you want a performance-based outcome, you should visualize yourself undertaking the steps necessary for creating that success - such as mentally picturing yourself perfectly executing any skills or process steps you need to undertake or master. The act of practice and rehearsal then help you prepare and then perform with excellence any skills or activities that need to be done.

PROCESS OR OUTCOME?

This distinction of whether you should focus on visualizing either a Process or Outcome was put to the test experimentally by researchers Pham and Taylor (1999) who had students either (1) visualize the ultimate goal of doing well in an exam, or (2) visualie the actual steps they would take to reach the goal of doing well, which meant studying, or (3) not using visualization at all.

It turns out that the study participants who visualized themselves going through the Process steps of studying to gain the required knowledge for an exam spent a longer time actually studying than the Outcome visualizers or the non-visualizers. They also started studying earlier than those who simply visualized getting an A on the exam.

In general, if a group of students started studying earlier and longer than others then on average you would expect that group as a whole to get higher exam grades. Of the two groups, those who visualized the Process did indeed get the best grades in the exam (an average of eight points better on the exam than non-visualizers) although the Outcome visualizers also increased their scores to a minor extent.

While there are also benefits to visualizing an Outcome you want, a quick conclusion is that it is far better to focus on visualizing yourself as a better performer of the Process that leads to a result than visualizing yourself as possessing the desired Outcome. This is because *you can only control your actions and not the results of your actions, and by improving your actions (through visualization and other efforts) you definitely increase your chances of attaining the outcome you want.*

A wise conclusion is that visualizing yourself as becoming the best you can be (while also feeling your internal energy along those lines), even when it stretches you out of your comfort zone, is often far better than visualizing that you are better than everyone else in terms of skills. Don't keep comparing yourself to competitors but strive to be so excellent that your level of performance is a thing in itself that others will look up to as a model for achievement. You should try to become the very best you can possibly be, and hopefully that "best" is so good that others cannot ignore you. You don't have to be the *absolute best* among the bunch for there will always be someone who comes along that is better. That is the nature of the universe, which is why all performance records of excellence are eventually broken.

You just have to ignite the fire to become the best you can be, and should strive to be outstanding such that others cannot ignore you. Try to be great and remarkable without peers. Try to be one of the immortals. Sometimes circumstances will limit how good you can ever become and there will always be someone better at whatever you excel at, but always reach for becoming the best you can become.

Advertising legend David Ogilvy once advised in a 1977 interview with John Chrichton: "Be more ambitious. Don't bunt. Try to hit the ball out of the park every time. Compete with the immortals. Try to make whatever you do the greatest that anyone has ever done. You won't always succeed but reach for the stars. Don't bunt. Be more ambitious. Ambition is the key. Try to do remarkable things. Try to be great. It is the lack of ambition that cripples most people." A motivating inspiration you should consider developing is to "be so good that others cannot ignore you."

Visualization is a tool that can help you reach such personal heights if you learn to master this skill.

In another Process-Outcome study by Pham, Taylor and others from 1998,[2] the researchers took eighty-four college students who had to complete a project into three groups: a control group, a Process visualization group, and an Outcome visualization group. The idea was to test how effective visualization work might be for planning efforts.

Over a one-week period, for five-minutes each day the group of Process visualization students visualized the action steps needed to complete a specified project. Over the same period, students in the Outcome visualization group visualized themselves as feeling pleased for having successfully completed the project. Students in the control group performed no visualization practice at all.

At the study's end, the control group of students who didn't use visualization had performed the poorest. Students in both the Process and the Outcome visualization groups were more likely to act earlier and begin the project on time than the control group, so visualization exercises helped both the Process and Outcome groups execute the process better. However, the Process group students who visualized the steps needed to complete the project were significantly more likely than the other groups to finish on time. Furthermore, Process visualizers generally considered the assignment easier than did students in the other groups. As to starting on time, the Process and Outcome visualizers were both better at this than the control group, but not much different from one another in this respect.

With these studies, how can you explain the results of Jim Carrey, Arnold Schwarzenegger, John Gray and Jack Canfield?

Napoleon Hill and other motivational experts might argue that visualization practice programmed their minds to help them maintain the motivation for achieving their goals, which sometimes lags when we are pursuing long-term objectives. It might also have helped them proceed through the process steps they had chosen were necessary for their success too.

In the examples given above of Jim Carrey, Arnold Schwarzenegger, John Gray and Jack Canfield, don't you think that the goals they envisioned for themselves, and their habit of mentally running through the process

[2] Taylor, S.E., Pham, L.B., Rivkin, I.D., & Armor, D.A. (1998). Harnessing the imagination: Mental simulation, self-regulation, and coping. American Psychologist, 53, 429-439.

steps to be executed with perfection, gave them an edge over other people who were also working towards those goals, but whose motivations might have swayed? Who was probably more prepared or more likely to execute each step of the process with excellence?

It seems that visualization practice has a power similar to vows, prayers or affirmations in the sense that it reminds us to take the action steps we need to take, without errors, in order to move ahead and achieve what we want. It helps us rehearse our performance in those steps, and helps us keep our goals fresh in our mind on a daily basis so our interest and motivation don't lag.

We must not forget, however, that visualizing a materialized Outcome that you already have achieved does not make our goal automatically manifest itself. There is no such thing as "magical manifestation" such that the universe pulls a desired result to you; you must work for it. It does not, through some mysterious process involving "attraction principles," make that goal easier to manifest through karma either. Rather, it builds inside your brain a pattern of achievement for what you are after. Having a mental blueprint of activity makes it more likely you will follow the plan effectively simply because (1) your actions always follow your thoughts and (2) through mental repetition an optimized plan can become a dominant aspiration you continually work towards achieving.

Remember that *there is no guarantee that your actions will ever produce the results you want in life*. However, you can and should use any and every tool possible at your disposal to achieve your life goals including visualization, mental rehearsal, visual thinking, mental imagery, inner energy work, focus and concentration. Use everything possible to help yourself achieve the outcomes you want in life, but don't attribute any magic to these activities. Visualization is only mentally rehearsing an outcome you want and creating a mental model of perfection you can strive to follow. It cannot magically manifest it.

In life you can only work at bettering your execution of a process (a performance) that produces a result. That being the case, you need to be sure that the Process steps you are executing constitute the *best and wisest* course of action for the outcome you desire. You cannot achieve a goal if the path you are following is deficient.

The way to then maximize your chances of achieving an outcome you envision is by getting good, getting better, or getting excellent at the process steps that would normally take you there. As with public speaking, stock trading or playing the violin, you cannot get better at a skill just by reading about it. You have to practice, practice, practice. For instance, visualization will help you learn the skills of playing the violin, but you also need to do the actual physical work of moving your fingers. Visualizing that you are an excellent speaker can help you build your confidence and mentally rehearsing your speeches will help you master your materials, but at the end of the day you must actually go out and make a speech. You must do whatever you envision. Visualization power may help you prepare and train yourself, but nothing actually happens until you work hard at the actual real-life process too.

The four people mentioned as success stories in this chapter were *fanatically* devoted to the Process of preparation and achievement, which is why they attained what they wanted. They never gave up going after what they wanted. They beneficially incorporated visualization routines into part of the Process that took them to their desired Outcome, but it certainly was not the only or most important part of their success Process.

While studies document a marked advantage to visualizing Process over Outcome because this emphasis helps you get things done, the strong motivation that comes from continually visualizing an outcome can inspire your actions and help maintain a burning desire to achieve some particular goal. As with self-talk, visualization practice can be a big confidence builder that helps you in a positive way.

To this point, heavyweight boxing champ **Muhammad Ali** explained that it was always important to mentally see himself victorious long before an actual boxing fight. Seeing himself victorious helped build his confidence, as did his verbal sparring.

Muhammad Ali also learned how to block out mental images representing doubt. If an image of difficulty or loss pops into the head of the top-tier professional athletes, they have usually trained themselves to become extremely adept at changing the internal movie, quickly editing the scene to imagine success. Ali used different mental practices to enhance his performance in the ring such as visualization and mental rehearsal. In order to boost self-confidence through self-talk, he also continually used the affirmation "I am the greatest" during his boxing career.

Many people say that the mental focus of top sports performers centers on two key elements - mental visualizations and self-talk. To perform at peak levels you must mentally train at visualizing an athletic skill with perfect execution and during its actual performance must use positive self-talk to banish wandering thought chatter, build concentration, and eliminate negativity. Visualizing scenes of success in your mind, or emotionally recalling positive feelings of achievement, can also be used.

Actor **Will Smith** is another notable who has said he regularly uses the power of visualization *and belief* to achieve goals that he sets. Internal belief is another mental factor we can purposefully develop that helps build confidence and moves us ahead.

Belief can be supported not just by developing your skills but by affirmations and positive self-talk as Ali demonstrated. The key to their effectiveness is how you phrase your affirmations, which is by focusing on the positive possessive and avoiding negative emotions or connotations. The right way to talk to yourself is therefore to say "I keep my exercise commitments" rather than "I never miss an exercise class." Another example of a proper affirmation to help stop smoking is to think "I'm proud of being committed to breathing only clean air" rather than "I don't have the desire to smoke cigarettes," which essentially might be repeating a lie. Affirmations should always be phrased positively with emotional passion and in the possessive. Unfortunately, the ins and outs of affirmations are not a topic we can go into deeply although they do support visualization efforts.

Highly successful people who do practice affirmations and mental imagery together, and who visualize the success they want over and over again know it doesn't guarantee the outcome they want, but it does help them work towards that result, and working hard towards an outcome we want is what matters.

The take-away conclusion for your life is that there isn't any magical role that visualization plays in manifesting results, but it does help people act in rehearsed ways that might bring them about. It helps you bring your actions to fruition, so in that sense helps you to materialize the results you want. These four notable individuals were among those who were able to actualize the results they wanted while using visualization as a helpful tool in their overall process.

Success won't somehow spiritualistically manifest due to the use of visualization in your life. Visualizing in itself will not, through some not-yet-understood set of universal laws, manifest an opportunity or Outcome for us. However, the visualization practice of mental rehearsal will be a positive tool to help keep you on track and in line with your desired objectives.

SELF-HELP ADVICE

Books like *Creative Visualization*, *The Magic of Thinking Big*, *The Magic of Believing*, and *Psycho-Cybernetics* all stand behind Napoleon Hill's idea in *Think and Grow Rich* that before you achieve anything of importance you must clearly define what it is that you want. You should vividly imagine it. You should clearly see it in your mind. You should visualize any end goal you seek in all its details.

If you want to practice visualization to help you achieve your goals, whatever they might be, there are several aspects to the practice to keep in mind such as the following:

Intensity

Experts say that the more real the mental visualization pattern you build the better your neural brain circuits will be that are involved with the subject and its context. When doing visualization practice, you should therefore try to generate as much detail as possible around the main event. Furthermore, adding emotion to your visual picture and various sensations along with it will help it become more real in your mind.

In fact, whenever you use visualization you should try to create Outcome images that involve inputs from all your senses of seeing, hearing, feeling, tasting and touching. Just as neuro-linguistic programming (NLP) teaches, when visualizing your goal you should include as many senses as possible in your imagination. In other words, try to make your mental imaging polysensual.

Frequency

For visualization practice to be helpful you need to refresh the mental image you build on a frequent basis. Just as you must continually refresh your commitment to a goal and fan your enthusiasm to keep it alive, it is useful to practice visualizations on a daily basis to strengthen your skills and commitments to that project.

Napoleon Hill suggested that people practice visualizing their success by creating vivid images every night before they go to sleep. He felt people should play them repeatedly like a movie in their mind before sleeping. Visualizing in this manner is simply a type of mental preparation and rehearsal, and the fact that you do it in the evening helps prepare your subconscious mind to work on the topic while you sleep.

The truth is that the more frequently you create a clear mental picture of your desired process steps, end result or very best performance you want to duplicate, the easier it will be for your brain to build the right neural circuits for duplicating the relevant achievement.

Therefore it is better to visualize goals or Processes frequently. If you are serious about success and want to make a serious change in your life or circumstances, you should set aside a specific visualization session during the course of the day. You might also adopt the habit of practicing your visualizations several times per day in short 2-5 minute bursts. This might sound like a very short time but you must remember that a football quarterback might quickly go through a play in his mind before calling it for the team, and just before taking a swing a tennis player might take a few seconds to visualize themselves hitting the perfect serve exactly in the place they want.

Practice Session Length

As to the length of time in visualization practice that you should practice holding a mental picture, some people can hold a mental picture for several seconds and some for several minutes. It all depends upon one's degree of concentration skills. For better results you need to practice longer and with more frequency. Since concentration is a skill that can be learned, the amount of time you can hold a stable image in your mind is a good measure of your ability. This length of time can easily be lengthened with practice. This is what you want – to practice being able to hold a stable image in your mind for longer and longer periods of time.

The amount of time you can hold a visualized image in your mind does not correlate to your chances of goal achievement. However, that length of time is a measure of the strength of your concentration muscles, and the ability to concentrate and keep at a goal will increase your chances of success and achievement. In a sense, your ability to concentrate and stay with a challenge – the characteristic we call grit or perseverance – are abilities directly related to success. Since concentration and perseverance can be developed through visualization practice, one can make the case that developing visualization skills can help you become successful because they help you develop your powers of concentration.

Learning how to concentrate without distraction can pay dividends in many ways. The longer you can hold a stable mental picture in your mind without wavering, the greater the concentration skills that you will be developing for staying on a topic, which you can readily use elsewhere in life to good benefit.

When practicing, the rule is that you should try to hold an image for as long as possible until your mind tires. After it tires, you should release the imaging session, empty your mind and rest (without holding onto anything any longer) -like a runner who takes a break after completing a strenuous race. During that resting period, try not to attach to any thoughts that arise. Ignore the sensations of internal energy that might arise, too, or alternatively you can use just a tiny bit of effort to smoothen them out and then rest in a state of empty mind where you observe them independently but ignore them too. Just witness everything that arises within your mind, and do so as if you were a bodiless observer. Just let your mind naturally function, and know everything within consciousness (thoughts, emotions, the environment) without forcing or attaching to any issue. At that point you should be like empty space that contains everything but you cannot attach to anything.

Experts always advise that you should visualize mental imagery with many sensory details, and in some cases this means it might take a long time to create an accurate visualization in your mind, so plan your practice sessions accordingly.

If you are using visualization practice to help with some type of performance, such as trying to improve a golf swing or improve your skiing skills at a particularly dangerous turn in a race you will have to visualize yourself performing at your best or doing everything perfectly at a skill level you do not yet have. However, since the entire real world performance may take a lot of time you will probably want to use some editing to emphasize visualizing just the important points to the process most relevant to your success.

Outcome or Process?

In *Think and Grow Rich*, Napoleon Hill states that you must know the steps leading to your life goals and should visualize working through them. You must clearly know the goals or objectives you are committing to (Outcome) as well as what you must do to attain them (Process), and then visualize yourself performing those steps (Process) and getting to that final Outcome.

During visualization practice you should see yourself performing the actions for becoming successful (Process) and actually achieving the successful Outcome you want. Both are beneficial visualizations, and both should be practiced but Process is what you should emphasize. Furthermore, *you should practice seeing this from both an External and Internal perspective.*

Don't just concentrate on visualizing an Outcome state because it is a Process that will take you there. You cannot just read a diet book, for instance, and then expect to lose weight. If you never go through the proper Process steps of achievement then you will never get to the Outcome, so you must concentrate on executing a process correctly.

Remember that you can use visualization practice to help you develop your *business skills* or learn how to *handle all sorts of everyday situations* that are due to arise in life, like learning how to answer the phone in a better fashion or ask a girl for a date. By frequently visualizing the Process steps you must take, the regular mental rehearsal with imagery will allow your mind to start creating solutions to your upcoming challenges that will help you gain mastery before the situation arises. You can certainly rehearse your skills through mental imagination and gain familiarity and proficiency with the outcome you are after.

Seeing something internally before you try it in real life often lets you realize whether or not you are headed in the right direction. Therefore sometimes visualization efforts allow you to avoid a lot of misplaced effort because you get to "try out" something before you take real action.

You can certainly create images in your mind of having achieved a particular goal (Outcome) or picture yourself executing a perfect performance of some task (Process). You can visualize yourself doing whatever it is you want (Process) or having achieved whatever it is that you want (Outcome). In both cases, remember that you need to set aside some practice time to repeat these mental images in your mind every day.

Ultimately, the big benefit to visualization practice, however, comes from its ability to help you improve Process performance, which is why athletes depend upon it. They use visualization practice to condition their mind in such a way that after repeated practice their body automatically behaves the way they want it to perform – in perfect fashion – *automatically without effort.* In that way they not only gain automatic skills that can make them unconsciously competent or even excellent, but also gain confidence in those skills as well.

LEARNING TO VISUALIZE

From this discussion you should now realize that effective visualization practice is not just wishful thinking, nor does it entail only brief moments of seeing yourself successful in your mind using mental pictures. It has a definite purpose to it, and can be quite effective in helping you achieve or materialize your life goals. The beneficial powers of visualization to help you create an outcome you want are not anything mysterious, superstitious or supernatural.

Rehearsing in your mind also does not guarantee an outcome you want, but it creates the possibility for you to create that desired outcome. You must still physically work hard at creating a desired outcome you want and not expect that you can wish it to magically manifest itself.

As we will see with sports excellence, achievement in life depends on the process of cause and effect rather than some secret magic. Visualization does not set up a magical cause in the universe that must somehow mysteriously respond in kind to satisfy your desires. It does, however, change your brain in certain ways and helps you perform actions that will bring you closer to your goals if you work on the correct Process steps. It helps you develop a workable plan in the mind, helps with the follow through on the plan, and helps you perform the process steps quite well.

Basically, during visualization practice you should use your imagination to see yourself going through all the steps of becoming successful (Process) and actually being successful (Outcome). You should also practice seeing an External picture of yourself performing whatever it is you envision, and whenever relevant you should try to visualize everything from an Internal perspective that sees the Process and/or Outcome as if from within yourself looking outwards.

If you do this, then visualization practice can definitely help you make your dreams and desires come true.

You can certainly use visualization powers to help program your subconscious mind. It can be used to help you change your habits; just as with athletes, due to repeated visualizations eventually your behavior will tend to automatically conform to the images you repeatedly envision. If you visualize yourself becoming the person you want to be then you can move yourself in that direction.

It can help you maintain the necessary motivation to pursue your goals, and thus it prepares the way for you to achieve that very outcome.

By helping you become familiar and comfortable with some future state of achievement it can help you reduce your feelings of anxiety about going through the Process steps to get there because you have already seen yourself in those steps countless times in preparation.

Visualization can definitely help you master skills via the benefits of mental rehearsal, which is why athletes consistently use it. Repeated visualizations eventually enable actual behaviors to automatically conform to the images of peak perfection and excellence repeatedly envisioned. This is how visualization practice helps you develop skills at levels of excellence.

When you mentally rehearse running through the Process steps for some desired Outcome, you are creating a particular mental program. When the chance finally arises in real life to perform in the way you mentally practiced, so that you might "live it" through a genuine performance, you will certainly be better prepared than if you had not mentally practiced, and will probably be better at it than if you had not mentally rehearsed at all.

No one ever said that it is easy to learn how to create images in your mind – still or moving. Only with persistence can you master the skill of visualization, but in time the training effort will pay off.

At first you are likely to get zero results when you initially try to visualize things, but don't give up. If you keep up with the effort, after a few weeks you will start to see shapes and pictures just as you want although they might not be clear or stable. After several months of daily practice you will start to become able to create vivid, controllable scenes as if you were a movie director. As you master this skill you will learn how to visually manipulate things as you want in your mind. At this point the power of being able to simply visualize something becomes the capability of visual thinking.

The rule is as it is in ordinary life - practice makes perfect. The more deliberate the effort you put into it the better will be your results, but remember that building visualization skills takes time. It takes time and effort to build your visualization muscles just as it takes time to build your athletic muscles.

Is it worth the effort? Are visualization skills worth all the trouble of practice?

It has been definitely proven that any concentration or deep thinking efforts enter your subconscious mind and can produce visual solutions to your problems and challenges. Why not then use visualization practice as a means for developing concentration and embedding your subconscious mind with helpful images? Why not try to master the visual thinking skills you can control? Why not use them to help change your life? Visualization powers, once mastered, will be invaluable to you over the years in many different ways once you achieve them.

If you want to get really good at developing special skills, you should practice visualizing that you perfectly execute that specific skill you want to master. Also, when you imagine achieving a final goal, hold a mental picture of it and try to feel as if it were a real event occurring to you at that very moment. Engage all your senses to vividly visualize your mental image in polysensual detail. One of the scenes you should practice mental picturing should be the moment you achieve the goal, namely the Outcome. You should practice holding that image in your mind while you are in a state of concentrated focus.

If there were such a thing as higher heavenly powers that helped people achieve their goals, all this mental practice would certainly notify them with utter clarity what you are after. The only question is whether your goal is worthy of you and beneficial to humanity.

Visualization powers can be a valuable mental tool that help you make your dreams and desires come true. You can certainly use your visual imagination to affect your subconscious mind, change your habits, shape your life, and attract success through positive achievements. You can certainly use the power of visualization to help achieve a goal you want in life, so it can indeed help you materialize your dreams and desires once you also add in the actual real world efforts. For help along these lines I suggest the book *Quick, Fast, Done* or *Move Forward*.

The major question always comes down to the best way to practice visualization skills and we will obtain further guidance on these issues from the well-tested field of sports visualization.

Chapter 5
SPORTS VISUALIZATIONS

In sports psychology literature you will find that internal imagery, mental rehearsal, imagination practice or visualization are all synonyms for "the cognitive rehearsal of a task in the absence of overt physical movement." Basically, whenever we imagine ourselves performing an action in the absence of physical practice, we are using imagery, imagination or visualization.

Visualization, the ability to create pictures in your mind, is one of the most powerful tools that an athlete can use to help achieve their personal best. It is now so common that many sports psychology books offer entire instructional chapters on the effectiveness of various visualization techniques. Among other things, visualization efforts are commonly used by athletes to improve their performance at specific skills such as hitting a ball, skiing a hill, swimming a race, jumping an obstacle, or moving their body in a certain way.

For athletes, visualization practice is a type of active mental rehearsal of how they want things to be. Using visualization as a training technique invariably results in much better athletic performances so elite athletes everywhere are now using it to gain a competitive edge.

Legendary sports figures like Tiger Woods, Pele, Jack Nicklaus, Michael Jordan, Jerry West, Michael Phelps, and Muhammad Ali have all used visualization practice and mental imagery to improve their game because it indeed creates an advantage that adds an edge.

Visualization exercises in athletics started to become popular as a performance enhancer when the Soviets began using them back in the 1970s for world competitions. Nowadays countless athletes commonly employ this training technique. Seasoned athletes are commonly trained to form vivid, highly detailed mental images and run-throughs of their entire athletic performance while engaging all their senses in their mental rehearsal. They learn how to combine their knowledge of the sports venue, including their athletic skills and game strategies, with their mental rehearsals for excellence.

Does visualization practice *really* work at improving athletic performance or is this form of concentration practice just a bunch of fantasy imagination without measurable results? Has it actually been scientifically proven to help athletes with training and performance?

Research reveals that mentally rehearsing a sport using visualization imagery can often be as effective as actual physical practice, and that doing both is the most effective type of athletic practice of all. Many athletes do not yet use visualization practice as a training technique but studies show that doing so usually results in a much better performance outcome.

We already found this holds true in business and life in general such as for delivering a speech, asking for a raise, or any other situation that requires skill, preparedness and forethought. However, it is a big jump from sculpting a positive image of being a new self with new skills (and trying to live up to the image) to imagining that you win a sports tournament and actually do so.

Researchers say it works in sports because thought can stimulate the nervous system in the same way an actual event does. When you imagine yourself performing perfectly and doing exactly what you want with your motor skills, you physiologically create neural patterns in your brain just as if you had physically performed the same actions. Performing or rehearsing an event in the mind therefore trains it by creating neural patterns that can guide our muscles to do exactly what we want.

Mental training such as regular visualization rehearsals can definitely improve almost all our skills and fast-track us towards our goals, but let's restrict ourselves to just the sports field to see if there are any irrefutable benefits because they have been measured.

ATHLETES WHO HAVE USED VISUALIZATION

Championship golfer **Jack Nicklaus** has said that he would use mental imagery for every shot he took, each time visualizing his ideal body posture and how he would execute the stroke.

In his book, *Golf My Way*, he described how he always visualized his performance at the tee, writing: "I never hit a shot even in practice without having a sharp in-focus picture of it in my head. It's like a colour movie. First, I 'see' the ball where I want it to finish, nice and white and sitting up high on the bright green grass. Then the scene quickly changes, and I 'see' the ball going there: its path, trajectory, and shape, even its behaviour on landing. Then there's a sort of fade-out, and the next scene shows me making the kind of swing that will turn the previous images into reality and only at the end of this short private Hollywood spectacular do I select a club and step up to the ball."

Another great golfer, **Jason Day**, closes his eyes and also imagines the exact shot he wants during his pre-shot routine. Day once revealed that he practices Outcome visualization, for he continually visualized himself holding the trophy for the 2015 Farmers Insurance Open before winning it.

Arnold Schwarzenegger, who won the Mr. Olympia bodybuilding contest four times and the Mr. Universe contest five times, used visualization practice for both Process and Outcome purposes. He addressed Process by visually sculpting his muscles while exercising so that they would become the ideal shape he wanted. Like Jason Day, he addressed Outcome by visualizing that he won his contests, saying, "I visualized myself being and having what it was I wanted. Before I won my first Mr. Universe title, I walked around the tournament like I owned it. I had won it so many times in my mind that there was no doubt I would win it. Then when I moved on to the movies, the same thing. I visualized myself being a famous actor and earning big money. ... I just knew it would happen."

Former NBA great **Jerry West**, who is known for hitting clutch shots at the buzzer, once explained that what accounted for his ability to make the big shots was that he had mentally rehearsed making those same shots countless times in his mind.

NBA player **Steve Nash** also engages in imaginary movements before every free throw. Specifically, he steps up to the line and mimes a few imaginary free throws before taking the actual free throws. Is this imaginary visualization effective? Nash has achieved a career free throw percentage of .904, making him the NBA's all-time leader in free throw percentage.

Nolan Ryan, baseball's all-time leader in strikeouts and no-hitters said, "The night before a game I lie down, close my eyes, relax my body, and prepare myself for the game. I go through the entire lineup of the other team, one batter at a time. I visualize exactly how I am going to pitch to each hitter and I see and feel myself throwing exactly the pitches that I want to throw. Before I ever begin to warm up at the ballpark, I've faced all of the opposition's hitters four times and I've gotten my body ready for exactly what it is I want to do."

Wade Boggs, one of baseball's best hitters, revealed that he would go into a preparatory "quiet time cocoon" for 15-20 minutes before each game. During that time he would focus on the pitcher and mentally deduce how he might try to get Boggs out, but Boggs "would envision getting a hit off the pitcher."

Ted Williams was one of the greatest hitters in baseball history with a

.344 batting average. In his book, *The Science of Hitting*, he explained that when batting he would mentally divide the strike zone into a quadrant composed of 77 discrete color-coded compartments, each of which was the size of a baseball. He would only swing at pitches when the ball entered a compartment where he could get a hit a high percentage of time. Knowing that a strike was better than swinging at a bad pitch, which could result in an out, he would patiently wait for the right pitch, waiting through strikes on the fringe of his best connecting zone. Williams' power of visualization and his self-control enabled him to become the last player ever to hit .400 for an entire season (he batted .406 in 1941).

Atlanta Braves' pitcher **John Smoltz** experienced a great turnaround in his baseball career when he finally learned to visualize his past successes while on the mound and bring the emotions associated with those prior successes into his present reality. The turnaround is understandable since imagining the peak performance of past successes helps evoke positive emotions that can lead to superior performance. Visualizing previous successes is actually easier than imagining something new because you already have the perfect success scenery in your memory.

Brazilian soccer player **Pele** is another athlete who would practice visualizing success an hour before every game. During his visualization routine he would go through a mental movie of his entire soccer life starting with him playing soccer as a child and ending with him reliving the best moments of his career at the World Cup. He would remind himself of the fun he felt playing as a young boy and try to bring those evoked emotions into his present state so that he could use that entrainment for the upcoming game.

STIMULUS OR RESPONSE?

Pele's case shows that positive emotions can propel athletic performance. They can act as a beneficial stimulus that will support the physical responses we want. If you keep a "mental game journal" of your best performances like Pele, through frequent visualization practice you can even learn how to evoke the corresponding positive emotions of those events at will so that you can use them during a competition.

Most visualization practice focuses on perfecting a particular motor skill that we can consider an Outcome or Response, and entails mental images of an optimal motor program for what you should do in a particular scenario. The visualized imagery is like a program on how to overtly respond to a situation. However, if used to train your emotions then mental imagery can also be used as a Stimulus vehicle rather than as just a mechanism to train motor responses. Using it in this way you can train yourself to recall (relive) arousing sensations as necessary. This ability to summon arousing emotions at will can provide you with an extra edge in crucial situations, such as in sports where tiny differences separate the champions from the losers.

In other words, if you richly combine visual, auditory, tactile, and kinesthetic images with emotions when creating your mental pictures, this "composite image" can more effectively evoke the emotions associated with desired behaviors. The closer your mental imagery mirrors realism – including the corresponding emotions - the easier it will be to interact with those images as if they were the real world. Such composite images can be used to evoke the proper responses you desire including psychophysiological changes in your body.

Putting it another way, visualization can be used to artificially (mentally) generate emotional states on call such as the emotional arousal that leads to peak performance. Therefore in addition to the Process-Outcome or Internal-External dimensions of visualization practice, we also have its possible usage for Stimulus or Response. This Stimulus-Response axis is another type of visualization training target we might employ.

In visualization practice you should always vividly picture the mental imagery with as much emotional color as possible, which will increase your ability to call on stimulating emotions as needed during any performance. The emotions you might choose to master could include motivation, arousal, endurance, courage and confidence. If you practice rehearsing sensory imagery with emotional intensity, you can learn how to bring such emotions to the table as a beneficial stimulus whenever they are needed.

As an example, golfer **Jordan Spieth's** coach once credited a portion of his tournament win at Augusta to the image reel they had created showing Jordan's best shots, which he was taught how to recall as a peak performance stimulus during play.

Gold medal Olympic swimming champion **Michael Phelps** learned how to use visualization techniques from his coach, Bob Bowman. After each session of swimming practice, Michael would go home and before falling sleep and upon waking would follow his coach's instructions to "watch the videotape" of a perfect race imagined in his head. Phelps had to mentally visualize the perfect race in exact detail, with each swimming movement being executed flawlessly with perfection. In conjunction with his intense physical practice, his visualization exercises helped him achieve Gold medals and world records during the 2008 and 2012 Olympic games.

Michael Phelps trained by not only seeing the perfect race in his mind, but would also imagine going through disaster scenarios of things not going well such as his goggles breaking or his suit ripping. He would regularly visualize a variety of adversity scenarios so that he already had a plan for any contingency that might happen to him during a race.

This is important because the most successful athletes work out good adaptation and coping skills for staying in control in the face of problems, such as when they might rip their uniform, become injured or receive an umpire's adverse call. They mentally rehearse how to handle problematic outcomes that have occurred in the past or are possible in the future, and have been coached to visualize positive outcomes during an event whenever adversity arises. In this case, Phelps mentally rehearsed all the possible calamities that might happen to him in a race and through visualization worked to create new neural pathways that would handle them should they occur.

Coach Bowman once explained that Phelps has all of these possible outcomes in his mental database so that when he swims a race he has already programmed his nervous system to react in one of those ways, and he'll just pick the one that happens to be necessary. Bowman explained that if everything is perfect then Phelps will just go with the perfect routine, but if he has to make any sort of change then he's already got the "programming" in there. Because of his extensive visualization practice Phelps never has to worry about adapting on the day of a competition but can focus solely on winning.

Sprint canoeist **Thomas Hall** is another Olympic athlete who attributed his success to his visualization practices. He was an underdog during the Beijing 2008 Olympics who was not expected to win any metals, but he ended up finishing in third place with a Bronze medal. He attributed this accomplishment to his diligent pursuit of visualization and mental rehearsal practices.

Olympic diver **Greg Louganis** achieved double gold medals in back-to-back Olympics due to his work at goal setting and visualization practice too.

Actually, 90% of Olympic athletes report that they now engage in visualization training efforts. It seems that athletes in all sports and at all levels of competition have commonly incorporated visualization and mental imagery into their training routines.

Marathon champion **Mark Plaatjes** also used them to help him win the IAAF World Championships marathon gold medal in 1993. While preparing for that race, Plaatjes practiced visualization techniques so much that he knew every undulation on the course and had "run" every possible scenario of the race in his mind before ever arriving in Stuttgart, Germany where the race was to be held. During the real race, Plaatjes's mental preparation helped him to snatch victory from the likely winner just three minutes from the finishing line. As a result, he became the first American to win a gold medal in a long-distance running event at the World Championships.

STUDIES OF VISUALIZATION'S IMPACT ON THE BRAIN

While all of these famous athletes have used visualization, mental imagery and mental rehearsal, each focused on different techniques because there are many types of visualization practice for sports training.

One visualization method is to create a perfect picture of just one particular aspect of a performance in your mind. You can also mentally rehearse an entire perfect performance too.

As before, the image might be created from an Internal perspective (by imagining what it looks like from the athlete's own eyes as the performance unfolds) or from an External perspective (by imagining the crowd's perspective of the athletic performance). If you were to imagine running a race then for the Internal view you would imagine seeing what you would experience on the course through your own eyes and for the External view you should practice seeing yourself running the race as if you were watching a video of yourself performing the activity.

You might also visualize something completely different than the actual performance such as the environment of the event (so you gain familiarity and confidence in what's upcoming) or the moment of victory with you as the winner.

The remarkable feature of visualization work is that when you regularly practice mental rehearsals according to certain principles, this can produce definite physiological changes in your body. Your mind can indeed transform your physical body, and specifically mental imagining can change your brain structure. When you mentally rehearse an activity through visualization practice you end up building a set of neural patterns in your nervous system along with a network of mental programs that can trigger physiological responses.

Shakyamuni Buddha taught this thousands of years ago in the *Surangama Sutra* when he said that you could provoke a physiological response in your body simply by thinking of the sour taste of a lemon or thinking about something fearful like walking on the edge of a cliff. He said that your aggregate of mental conceptions could affect the aggregate of sensations/feelings for your body-mind complex, which could in turn affect your physical body because of an inter-linkage between these systems. In the *Surangama Sutra* he provided the world with one of the first in-depth discussions of the mind-body connection.

Volleyball

A 1998 article in the *European Journal of Applied Physiology* ("Autonomic nervous system responses correlate with mental rehearsal in volleyball training") confirmed the mind-body connection affected by visualization practice, which also has implications for how we can change our thoughts to transform the body. The study identified six unique autonomic nervous system responses that correlated with visualized mental rehearsal: heart rate, respiratory rate, skin temperature, skin heat clearance, skin potential and resistance.

The researchers (R. Roure, C. Collet, C. Deschaumes-Molinaro, A. Dittmar, H. Rada, G. Delhomme, E. Vernet-Maury) studied the athletic task of a volleyball player passing an opponent's serve to a teammate. Participants performed the task both physically and through visualization. Both provoked similar responses in the nervous system! The investigators concluded that your mental imagery – fashioned through visualization practice – could help construct schema that could be reproduced, without thinking, in actual real world practice. In other words, visualization practice could help to build mental blueprint patterns that could become automatic behavioral responses.

Weight Lifting

Other research, using an EEG (electroencephalogram) machine that measures brain waves, has also shown that the electrical activity produced by the brain is identical whether we are thinking about doing something or actually doing it.

One study involving weight lifters showed that the brain patterns activated during lifting were similarly activated when the lifters just visualized themselves lifting the weights. The surprising finding was not the mind-body connection, but that the visualized mental rehearsal was nearly as effective as physical practice for strength building!

EEG patterns in the brain that would normally be activated when lifting several hundred pounds were also activated just by imagining that you were lifting that weight. Thoughts alone, created through visualized imagery (visualization practice), were enough by themselves to produce the neural instructions that executed the act.

What was an even more important finding from this study was that doing both – actual physical practice and visualization practice - constituted more effective lifting practice than performing either solo. This is why coaches advise athletes to perform both physical and mental practice together. An August 2005 study in France, published in *Perceptual and Motor Skills*, also confirmed that practicing mental imagery combined with physical practice greatly improves performance, with improvement occurring even with beginning athletes.

Skiing

In another study done by sports psychologist Richard Suinn, a group of skiers were wired to special EMG (electromyography) equipment to test their neuromuscular responses while they were carrying out mental rehearsals of skiing. As the skiers mentally rehearsed downhill runs in their minds, visualizing everything they must do to run a successful course, the electrical impulses heading to their muscles while visualizing were found to be the same as those they used in real life while actually skiing the run.

Even though the skiers weren't moving, the exact same muscles they would have used during a downhill ski were being activated because of using their mind.

Just as with the weight lifters and volleyball players, the brain sent the same instructions to the body when the skiers were simply thinking of making jumps and turns as when they were actually carrying them out. Visualized behavior, namely thoughts (conceptions), produced the similar mental instructions and physiological responses as actions did.

WHY VISUALIZATION WORKS

Basically, the science shows that whenever an athlete imagines performing a particular sports activity, his muscles fire in the same sequence they would if he were actually physically performing the same movements.

From this finding you might conclude, as others have, that because of our mental processes and physiological responses our brain processes the input from imagined and real experiences in a similar fashion.

This sort of psycho-neuromuscular theory explains how visualization practice strengthens the neural pathways for movements that you imagine making, and why visualization can therefore be used in various types of performance training. Mental rehearsal basically creates the neural patterns necessary for the real behavior you desire.

The idea behind using mental imagery for performance training is that forming metal images in your mind will help construct schema (mental and physiologically) which can be reproduced, almost automatically, in actual life. Repeated mental rehearsal of visualized movement imagery (together with other sensory feelings) will therefore help you create the neural pathways necessary for manifesting the real thing. Visualization practice can help you create and then strengthen a "mental blueprint" in your brain, so using it is like carving a groove into your nervous system, enabling your actions/movements to become more automatic.

Let's compare the results of visualization practice with purely physical exercise and the physical biochemistry of motor movements. When an athlete performs a muscular function the signaling neurotransmitters in the muscles are stimulated along a particular pathway, and the chemicals that have been produced remain there for a short period. If there is any future stimulation along the same pathways, the difficulty of treading that particular pathway is reduced due to the residual effects of the earlier connections.

Putting it simply, the more you physically exercise in a certain way, the easier it becomes to repeat the same movements again. Not only have your muscle fibers been stretched in a certain fashion and your biochemistry altered but your neural pathways have been strengthened for those movements. The more we do something the more our neural connections, physical pathways and signaling mechanisms become hard-wired. We naturally become more skilled at physical tasks after these neural pathways and electrical signaling circuits are developed. If we therefore practice athletics with the view that the brain is just another muscle, mentally rehearsing athletic skills through visualization practice is a *must activity* since it will train our brain to facilitate the movements needed for actual performance.

If your body or mind has to select neural pathways to perform an action, it will usually select the familiar ones that have seen the most usage. This is why people normally default in behavior to their old habits, which is because the neural pathways associated with habits have been the ones most preferred over time. To create a new habit you cannot destroy an old set of pathways, but must forge new pathways for improved behavior. Then you must start using those pathways as your new preferred mode of acting instead of old pathways, in effect letting the previously used neural networks decline.

The neural traffic circuits for impulses which are automatically selected by your body-mind are usually the ones that have been used more often than other pathways. The greater usage has made them rather conspicuous like the grooves that form in a road due to a volume of excessive traffic. If you just follow habit energy, those are the circuits your behavior will usually conform to.

Scientists believe that the neural pathways commonly used develop thicker myelin sheaths that speed cellular communication, and this is why they become the preferred or dominant connection routes for nerve signals. The thicker myelin develops skills development which therefore forges thicker neural circuits. If you want to forge really excellent neural circuits, you are advised to adopt the training routine of deep, deliberate practice espoused in the works of K. Anders Ericcson, Geoff Colvin (*Talent is Overrated*) and Daniel Coyle (*The Talent Code*). These works are highly recommended.

Building a new skill to perfection (which means forging neural pathways that represent excellence) is like building a road in the wilderness to an entirely new location. That new skill will improve only by following the new road you build. The amazing thing is that because the brain doesn't distinguish between doing something and just thinking about doing it, mentally rehearsing the skill will lay down the road just as well as physical practice does. Imaginary rehearsals can therefore be just as effective for a novice learning a skill as actually performing the physical skill itself because imagining that you are doing the activity can also lay down proper neural pathways. In other words, visualization practice can help you build the right brain circuits just as does physical practice. Therefore you can use it to train yourself to a state of performance excellence.

When athletes are in the early learning phase of some skill, they are still figuring out what to do and how to do it. They are like a hiker lost in the wilderness without any tracks to follow. As they begin to understand how a skill should be properly executed, however, rehearsing it through visualization can help build the correct neural networks and signaling systems. That rehearsing can assist learners to perform a skill correctly.

Whether we physically perform an activity or only picture it in our minds, we are activating many of the very same neural networks in both instances; mentally imagining an activity activates the same neural pathways as those used in doing the physical activity itself. You can use this to your advantage in different ways, especially in training for sports excellence. For instance, just imagining yourself *perfectly performing* the particular movements required of your sport will help you get better at them.

Remember what Jack Nicklaus said, "I never hit a golf shot without having a sharp picture of it in my head. First I 'see' where I want the ball to finish. Then I 'see' it going there; its trajectory and landing. The next 'scene' shows me making the swing that will turn the previous images into reality." In other words, Nicklaus practiced each shot in his mind before taking it including exactly how he wanted his muscles to move.

When you imagine practicing a skill by visualizing it in your mind you strengthen the neural pathways in the brain required for that skill because you activate the same brain areas used in reality. The mental imaging strengthens the neural circuits you will need when it is time to perform and every time you mentally reinforce those (through mental imagery or real movement) you make those pathways a little bit stronger and *faster*.

Therefore it is important during mental training to imagine that any skill or talent you want to develop is executed with perfection because those are the pathways you will build. You make it more likely you will reproduce "perfection" in the future if it is "perfection" that you practiced visualizing.

Done consistently with regularity, visualizing a perfect performance in vivid detail helps you reliably "hard-wire" a great performance in your brain. When you practice these types of visualizations, the more details the better because the more real your mental image (the more vivid and complete your imagination) the more convinced your brain will be that this is real life, and then the neural patterns you create will be better at teaching your muscles to do exactly what you want.

Visualizing an effort hundreds or thousands of times will create just as many correct neural linkups as pure physical practice, and envisioned perfect movements will start to guide your physical movements after a while. Once a perfect mental pattern has developed due to mental rehearsals, you can start to automatically rely on it during real performances.

When you repeatedly visualize performing some athletic skill, you can condition yourself so that an improvement feels familiar when you actually perform it. This can help make your actions more automatic as well as build confidence.

Did you ever notice how elite athletes remain calm under pressure? That's not just due to all their physical training, but because they have already ran through every possible scenario in their minds before stepping onto the field. Because of prior visualization work, they normally have greater confidence than others since they have less need to think in pressure situations but can just react.

Despite all the benefits from visualization practice, visualizing the perfect performance doesn't replace the necessity for doing hard work in actual practice. However, when done in tandem with consistent, intelligent practice effort (especially "deep" practice and "deliberate" practice) you maximize the chances for an excellent performance.

STUDIES OF VISUALIZATION PRACTICE ON PERFORMANCE

There is no doubt that visualization skills can be an amazing performance enhancer that allows you to acquire and perfect physical skills much more quickly. You've already encountered the stories of quite a few athletic greats who used visualization routines and credited their success to it, but could that attribution just be their imagination? Where is the proof or evidence?

A number of scientific studies are also available that demonstrate objectively the positive impact that visualization has on performance, confirming its effectiveness for physical training.

Russian Olympics

The Soviet Union used visualization practice to prepare its teams for the 1980 Olympics. To better understand how to improve performance, a study was done where athletes were split into four groups, each of which devoted itself to a different amount of visualization practice.

Group 1 used 100% traditional physical practice without any visualization efforts. Group 2 employed a schedule of 75% physical practice and 25% mental practice. Group 3 used 50% physical and 50% mental practice, while Group 4 devoted itself to 75% mental and 25% physical practice.

After the Moscow and Lake Placid Olympics a tally of athlete scores surprisingly showed that those in Group 4 had won the most medals.

Colorado Olympic Training

In another Olympic-related study conducted at the Olympic Training Center in Colorado, thirty-two golfers practiced their putting skills every day for one week.

A first group visualized all their golfing physical motions and the ball going into the hole because of their putt. A second group visualized the ball veering away from the cup. A third group performed regular putting practice without any visualization efforts at all.

The final results were that the putting skills of the visualizers increased by 30%. Those who visualized the ball missing the cup saw their putting accuracy go down by 21%, while those who simply practiced putting skills in the normal way saw their accuracy go up by 11%.

Such is the power of visualization at improving outcomes.

Field Hockey

Similarly, a 1991 study of 121 field hockey players also found that players who just did physical practice improved their shooting skills, in this case by 70%, while those who used visualized imagery *in addition to* their physical practice improved their goal shooting by the far higher amount of 160%.

Basketball

In a famous basketball study, one team practiced shooting basketballs for four hours per day. Another team practiced shooting for three hours and visualized making perfect shots for just one hour. After tallying results, the study found that the second team scored 26% more than the first due to the addition of its visualization practice.

Another basketball study, conducted by Dr. Biasiotto at the University of Chicago, split people into three groups to test their free throwing skills. Biasiotto had one group physically practice free throws every day for an hour without using any visualization efforts. A second group were to just visualize themselves making free throws, but didn't do any physical practice. A third group acted as the control and did no type of practice at all.

Biasiotto measured how everyone did and after thirty days tested everyone again. He found that the first group improved their shooting by 24%, but the second group of visualizers improved by 23% without ever having touched a basketball! Amazingly, they achieved almost the same improvement without undergoing the physical exercise! The third group did not show any improvements in their shooting accuracy, which is what one would expect.

Had another group implemented both physical practice and the mental visualization the results would probably would have been best of all. In fact, Gaggioli, Morganti, Mondoni, and Antonietti conducted a study in 2013 that did combine mental and physical training for the lay-up shot in basketball. The results were exactly as you might expect, namely that mental practice improved coordination and movement accuracy for players practicing one of basketball's most complex motor skills. In short, it was found that mental imagery enhanced athletic performance.

Trampoliners

In 1992, Anne Isaac led an experiment with seventy-eight trampolinists. The group consisted of some experts and some novices. Dividing them into experimental and control groups, Isaac tested the participants on their visualization skills and classified them as either high or low imagers.

Both groups of participants were then trained in three trampoline skills over a six-week period. The practice session was always run as follows: (a) 2.5 minutes of physical practice on perfecting the skills, (b) 5 minutes of skill visualization practice for the experimental group, (c) 5 minutes of abstract mental problems (like math or some other metal puzzle) for the control group, and (d) 2.5 minutes of physical practice once more.

At the end of the study, there was a significant difference in performance between the high and low imager (visualizer) groups. As you might expect, the high imagers got superior results. There was also a significant difference in new skills between the mental imagery group which used visualization and the control group, where once again those who used visualization outperformed those who did not use it.

Isaac's study was a blind study where Isaac was unaware of who was in which group, and it clearly showed that not only was visualization successful, but better visualization led to more success in developing skills.

Isaac also found that *both the novice and expert groups saw improvement in their skills due to visualization practice,* which suggests that visualization can help both beginners and advanced performers alike. Another researcher (Pie, 1996) found that "… the more the subject is skilled and the more acquainted he or she is with the physical task, the greater probability of him/her achieving actual physical progress through internal imagery."

Muscle Strength

Guang Yue, an exercise psychologist from Cleveland Clinic Foundation in Ohio, also conducted a study to compare "people who went to the gym with people who carried out virtual workouts in their heads."

After testing two groups of people, he found that the group who physically went to the gym and worked out saw a 30% increase in muscle strength while participants who merely conducted mental exercises of the same weight training increased their muscle strength by almost half as much (13.5%). This strength gain due to visualization efforts even remained for three solid months following the mental training.

Another study in 2004 tested the results of visualization practices on strength training by splitting thirty healthy volunteers into separate groups. The first group performed physical training exercises with their little finger while the second group was trained to perform "mental contractions" of their little finger and simply imagined, through visualization, doing the same training in practice sessions. A third group was not trained but participated in all measurements to serve as a control group.

This training experiment lasted for 12 weeks (15 minutes per day, 5 days per week). The results were that the physical training participants increased their the finger abduction strength by 53%, while those who only mentally rehearsed the movements increased their finger abduction strength by 35%. The control group showed no significant changes in strength at all.

Once again the study showed that visualization efforts could help you increase your strength even without the accompanying exercises.

A visualization study from 2007 that appeared in the *North American Journal of Psychology* also found similar results. Practicing five times a week for 15 minutes per day, athletes who only mentally practiced a hip-flexor exercise using visualization achieved strength gains that were almost as significant as those achieved by people who actually did the exercise on a weight machine.

A study by Guillot, published in the *Journal of Strength and Conditioning Research* in 2010, found that people who visually imagined doing leg presses between sets were actually able to lift more weight and do more repetitions than those who didn't use visualization practices.

All in all, many studies definitively prove that visualization practice can help us increase our skills and change our body's abilities.

HOW TO STRUCTURE PRACTICE

From the many studies that have been undertaken, it is clear that mental imagery rehearsal is a very effective technique that helps athletes improve their performance and play at their best. Mental imagery, meaning visualization practice, can help an athlete in many areas of their sport, which is why most elite and professional athletes are already using mental imagery as part of their training routines. It is a tool that can lead to peak performance.

The main reason athletes practice visualization is because they want to condition their mind in such a way that the body automatically behaves the way they want it to without effort, which can take their performance to the next level of excellence. Visualization practice not only improves motor skills so that you become unconsciously competent at a model of perfection, but improves your confidence and reduces performance anxiety as well. If you want to achieve peak athletic performance, combining physical practice with visualization mental training seems to be the best method.

From a broad perspective, in general there are **five different types of imagery** that an athlete can try to master through visualization practice: (1) Imagery involving mentally rehearsing the execution of plans and strategies of play (2) Process imagery used in acquiring or improving skills that involves rehearsing those skills (3) Imagery centered around relaxation, stress reduction or reducing performance anxiety and arousal (4) Imagery used to summon confidence, the feeling of being in control or other emotional Stimulus necessary for top performance, and (5) Outcome or Results imagery involving the achievement of goals and accomplishments.

When visualizing these various types of situations, it is important that the type of mental imagery you choose matches the intended outcome you are after. For instance, if you want to improve your ability to hit a ball, you need to imagine yourself hitting all sorts of serves perfectly, without error, and sending the ball to exactly where you want it to go. If you want to improve your ability to catch a ball, you need to imagine yourself making all sorts of difficult catches. If you want to improve your speed, you need to imagine yourself as being speedier in the way that matters.

When using visualization techniques, you must vividly picture yourself performing the skill or routine 100% perfectly and confidently. Always imagine your task or skill is performed to *perfection without errors* in order to build the right neural circuits. Also, because every individual is different there is no one correct way to practice mental imagery. Internal and External imagery, as well as Process and Outcome or Stimulus and Results imagery, are all beneficial. The type of imagery to concentrate on developing depends upon your goals and situation. Many options are available and due to those many options, sports psychologists and game coaches therefore try to structure mental rehearsals for athletes in a way that gets the most benefit out of it.

Usually as a form of preparation top athletes will imagine an upcoming game from the Internal perspective of actually competing. They usually visualize mental trial runs of an event as if they are seeing the world outside their eyes. Furthermore, they try to employ all of their normal senses in their mental pictures.

The most successful type of athletic practice is to break down a skill or performance into tiny component pieces and work on perfecting those specific chunks before linking them back together into a larger whole. Internal and External visualizations are both used to develop the specific skills of athletic Process along these lines.

Athletes must also learn how to concentrate during the most difficult pressure-filled moments and need to work out good coping strategies for staying in control during adversity. To summon confidence and the feeling of being in control, athletes can use External and Internal imagery to train to develop coping pressure. Athletes can also use them to help them master the various strategies of play.

Visualization can be used to create visual imagery of circumstances that you want to occur in reality, so by all means visualize that you excel at whatever you wish to master and visualize becoming victorious in athletic contests. This will help you build familiarity and confidence with that end result, but you must also physically train for that victory as well since your physical skills produce the win. When visualizing victory, athletes can imagine it as if viewing an External motion picture, or as if experiencing it from within (Internal imagery) while feeling all their senses alive so as to build that familiarity and confidence. Emotional richness is difficult to initially incorporate into visualizations but with practice athletes can learn how to imagine (re-create) all of their normal senses in Process or Outcome visualizations.

It is a standard instruction of sports excellence coaches and others to engage all your senses during visualization practice. Try to imagine feeling, seeing, hearing, smelling and tasting everything – imagine experiencing your body, your movements, the setting, the competitors, the audience, and the internal feelings of confidence and power and knowledge you will be at your best. The power of mental imagery is that you can create a vivid image that not only includes the mechanics of the task but also the emotions that normally accompany it, *or the emotions that you want to go with it*. You can certainly use visualization practice to train your emotions to become the way you want, which is a method we saw was often used for seekers of business success.

For sports training, the most vital imagery type appears to be kinesthetic visualization where you mentally rehearse the "feel" of your performance. For instance, it was found that champion rowers are most successful when they can mentally "feel" all the parts of the race from the sitting to the oaring to their breathing and to the strain on their rowing muscles. Therefore for athletic training you should try to imagine feeling how you will move, matching it with your visual senses, in order to optimally develop the neural circuits of your brain.

Remember that "visualization," "mental rehearsal" or "imagery" does not just mean internal seeing, but engagement of all your emotions and senses. Your auditory, kinesthetic, olfactory and gustatory senses should all be welcomed within any visualizations you practice, especially the feelings of energy moving inside your body. When athletes are using mental imagery they should try to not only see but also to feel, hear, feel, taste and smell everything going on around them in the imagined situation too. As baseball hitter Ted Williams demonstrated with his 7x11 (77 sections) baseball grid, you can also learn how to project visualizations into the real world to help you achieve peak performance.

Employing your senses other than just sight and projecting visualizations into the real world might be even more important than seeing itself, but it depends upon the sport and athlete. Because some people are auditory or kinesthetic learners, such as many musicians, the most important task for a mental coach is to discover the person's dominant learning style or performance mode and teaching them through that channel of practice. In any case, a wide variety of visualization (mental imagery) options are available for people of all types.

Visualization can be practiced at any time or place, in any position and certainly over a long duration for the best results. You can practice in conjunction with music or in perfect silence. However you choose to do it, the point is that you should somehow work visualization power into your practice routine if you want to improve your athletic skills and game.

The major issues for coaches are how to structure visualization practice for the specific people you are coaching and how to apply the use of mental imagery in the real life sports settings to improve the performance of your athletes.

PERSONAL PRACTICE

So how do you personally become good at visualizing to improve your sports skills? Through practice. In short, you must practice both Process and Outcome imagery from both an Internal and External perspective. To learn how to master emotions you should also practice Stimulus-Response visualizations as well.

Let's take golf as an example. In a mental practice session you might actually see yourself going through the swinging Process of hitting the shot – seeing yourself executing a perfect stroke – while also imagining the flight of the ball going exactly where you want just as Jack Nicklaus would do. To learn how to execute the perfect golf swing, you would first purchase videos or DVDs of perfect swings by golf legends and then replay them over and over again until the images are burned into your memory and you can recreate them at will. Then during visualization practice it is a matter of imagining the feel, timing and pacing of the swing (along with your breathing and son on) just as you would expect to experience them in real life. Lastly, instead of externally imagining the golfer performing the swing you have to picture yourself doing it.

To visualize the Outcome of making a shot before you take it, you need to make a vivid picture in your mind of exactly what you want to happen. If you have practiced other types of visualizations where you learn how to project geometric figures on the external environment (*since you are actually just manipulating pictures in your mind*), you can now use that skill in real time for sports achievement.

As so many great athletes and coaches have said, "Sports is 90% mental and 10% physical" so there is a large role that visualization mental practice can play in helping you with your sports skills. Top athletes don't waste time on things that do not work, so it should come as no surprise that visualization can be a powerful tool for learning athletic skills, improving your performance, rehearsing strategies, adjusting emotions, correcting mistakes, focusing attention, blocking out distractions, reducing anxiety, increasing confidence, and just helping you excel and win.

Unfortunately, mental training techniques like visualization practice are rarely emphasized in youth sports when they should be. It is something that should be brought into the world in a big way. Few young athletes are taught that mentally imagining yourself doing movements in a perfect fashion can help you become better at executing them. Neither are they taught techniques, such as the NLP "circle of excellence" exercise, that train them to imagine themselves performing as the greatest athletes of all time. Visualization practice can be used in many ways such as helping you correct your bad habits and overcome mistakes that have been producing significantly bad consequences.

Because they aren't aware of its potential, many young athletes never reach their levels of peak performance or "flow" that it might be possible to reach if they were using the performance enhancement methods of mental imagery and visualization rehearsals.

If you want to play better in sports, then learn to visualize succeeding in your mind before you actually play. Visualize every detail of what you will be doing as well as everything that will go into having a "perfect" game or performance. Just as you can use visualization practice to rehearse the "perfect" speech, you can use it in sports training to help you outperform.

Visualization practice should be vivid, active and purposeful. It should involve all your senses. Remember, it works because when you imagine yourself performing perfectly and doing exactly what you want you will physiologically create neural patterns in your brain just as if you had physically performed those actions. Your thoughts, even though it is just your active imagination, can stimulate your nervous system in the same way that an actual event does. You can therefore use visualization practice for training purposes.

A SIMPLE EXERCISE

Let's go through a simple visualization exercise combined with a real sports training event to show how this all ties together.

Close your eyes.

Imagine yourself performing the perfect pitch, hit, run, swing, catch, snatch, squat, turn, or whatever you want to master.

Next, work through that practice in real time. Don't rush anything or skip any steps. *Execute with perfection exactly what you just imagined doing with perfection.* Slow down or speed up that execution in order to catch errors and correct them. Work on doing it properly and correctly until you achieve perfection, and then visually and kinesthetically memorize that state along with your body sensations. Thereafter, during visualization practice you can now play back those images and associated feelings in your mind to slowly perfect that skill without going through the physical motions.

If you are trying to perfect a level of excellence you have not yet achieved – such as learning a new tennis swing - you can use a visualization of that perfection in your mental playbacks as well, which is what most people practice doing. To improve your actual physical skills, repeat this mental playback as often as you can, and always visualize that you are performing with error-free perfection.

Sports psychology consultant Reggie Younger Jr. once wrote, "I had a track athlete who participated in the high jump event at his high school. He was having trouble achieving success in the sport by increasing his height and desired a personal best to move up in the standings. By using visualization (30 seconds) of successful clearance prior to his approach (run up) to the bar he was able to improve his height and move up in the standings to be in contention for the state title. The mental imagery technique used began from the approach to the bar, the lift of the jump through to the end so he was able to see the entire picture of success prior to each occurrence." This example from the VRC Sports Psychology Performance website shows how powerful it can be.

It might seem like science fiction, but if you simply imagine yourself regularly performing a skill perfectly, and you visualize it often enough, your brain will start to build circuits that allow you to repeat what you have imagined in the real world. This is the secret behind superior sports training.

If you're having trouble when you first start doing visualization practice, you can look at game videos or skill videos (ex. videos of perfect batting swings, golf swings, tennis returns, skiing turns, etc.) just prior to using your imagination. You can do this to build the perfect mental blueprint of the optimal pattern you wish to emulate.

When it comes time to practice mental visualizations, always remember to make your internal imagery as vivid and realistic as possible - including input from all your senses – to perfect the best brain circuits possible. Furthermore, only imagine perfection and never imagine producing an error. This will build the right brain circuits from the start and they will link what your body does to the brain impulses that control it. In always mentally imagining perfection, you will also boost your self-confidence and develop many types of advantage.

You should practice sports/athletic imagery as often as you can because it takes time for it to bring out your best. *It may take weeks or months* before you start to see any improvement in your skills and scores, so don't get discouraged if it seems that progress is coming slowly. Just as it takes time to build a muscle, it takes time to build the right neural circuits for athletic outperformance. Remember that when you visualize performance there are certain changes that must take place in your body and brain, and they will tend to occur even though you may be unaware of that process.

We have previously seen that visualization exercises can help anyone who desires increased success and performance. Highly successful people ("winners") in many fields use it, and various studies have certainly proven its reach and effectiveness.

Using visualization (mental imagery) practice will definitely create new neurological patterns in your brain that will help you move toward something new that you desire. If you visualize the success you want over and over again, eventually your body may be able to automatically conform to the image and make it a physical reality. There are multiple ways to practice inner visualization and in sports it can certainly help you to improve your performance and achieve your personal best.

Chapter 6
HEALING VISUALIZATIONS

We have seen from the sports visualization studies that mental imagery can improve movement skills and because it builds neural pathways it can even transform your physical body. The question therefore arises whether it can help with healing.

The answer is yes, and in fact it can even help you maintain your level of athletic capability while you recover from injury. However, an important point we should first cover is that doctors and surgeons, *like athletes* or inventors or mathematicians, businessmen and so on, can use visualization practice as a form of training to improve their skills. Surgeons, in particular, are known for visualizing their procedures as a type of preparation.

SURGEONS CAN IMPROVE THEIR SKILLS

For instance, **Dr. Charles Mayo,** who founded the Mayo Clinic, is well-known for mentally rehearsing all his procedures the night before an operation.

Similarly, **Dr. Teodor Grantcharov,** a laparoscopic surgeon at St. Michael's Hospital in Toronto, has used visualization techniques to optimize his operating room performance since his early days as a resident. He reports:

"I always wake up in the morning and I think for five, 10 minutes about the cases I have today and kind of imagine what kind of steps am I going to do. What am I going to do if this goes wrong? And it kind of prepares you mentally for the day. And suddenly I feel less stressed."

"I still do it every day when I'm in the operating room, and my own experience combined with evidence from other high-performance

66

industries like professional sports gave us the idea that this is something we'd like to study in a systematic way."

In a study published by the *British Journal of Surgery*, Grantcharov and a team of researchers examined whether mental practice could improve training for surgeons in laparoscopy (keyhole surgery) among third- and fourth-year residents who were training via a simulated operation. In his study, twenty surgical residents who were to learn the jejunojejunostomy (JJ) operation, which is one part of a gastric bypass surgery, were broken into two groups. One group of residents received conventional surgical training while the second group received surgical training along with mental practice training before performing a jejunojejunostomy operation on a pig.

The JJ is a technically challenging operation when performed with laparoscopy, which uses a scope-guided instrument that a surgeon manipulates while watching images on a computer screen. It requires "intracorporeal suturing," which is a hard skill to teach and difficult skill to master since it is the most advanced technique in laparoscopic surgery. Approximately 86% of the errors in laparoscopic surgery happen during two steps of this surgical procedure.

To determine if visualization practice could change the surgical error rate, the researchers gave half the surgical residents a "script" so they could mentally prepare for a week prior to the training operation on the pig. The script was produced from expert surgeons they could model who had described through interviews "how they do it and how they see and feel." It outlined every step of the procedure, which thus allowed them to repeatedly go through each step of the operation in their minds. They could then mentally practice the operation without actually doing it and learn which parts were more difficult or more stressful than others. This group also received imagery training from an experienced performance psychologist who worked with professional sports teams.

At the end of the study, the difference between the two groups proved beyond the shadow of a doubt that visualization works. The group that had visualization training was much better at performing the technical components of the surgery, and was even better prepared to handle an unannounced crisis scenario than those lacking the training. Visualization practice clearly works!

HEAL YOURSELF MENTALLY

If you are sick or disabled, you can also employ the same type of visualization practices and mental rehearsal techniques used by athletes to cure illness. Visualization is one of the many effective modalities that can help people with healing. In fact, the use of visualization and mental imagery has been used as a healing tool in many world cultures, which is an additional reason why it has become an integral part of many religions. The Navajo Indians, for instance, teach people to practice a special form of mental imagery for healing purposes where an individual "sees" himself as healthy.

Research over the last few decades has demonstrated conclusively that visualization can reduce your blood pressure, blood glucose levels, cholesterol, and increase your white blood cell activity. It can help reduce the adverse side effects of chemotherapy and radiation therapy (such as nausea, depression, and fatigue). It can lessen or eliminate headaches and pain, increase or decrease blood flow to areas of the body, and reduce your need for medications. It can reduce bleeding and shorten surgical recovery times. It can be used to reduce fear, stress and anxiety. It can also be used to stimulate our immune system. In short, it can beneficially influence many aspects of health and healing!

The evidence indicates that the power of visualization isn't just effective in helping people accomplish goals and improve skills, but can be used to promote good health and heal the body. In other words, the same mental rehearsal technique used by athletes can be effective in treating illness.

One common visualization practice for healing is to visually imagine your body fighting an illness or countering pain in order to boost the effectiveness of your treatments. This approach has been used in cancer treatment and cases of lower back-pain, high blood pressure, anxiety, depression, fibromyalgia and other conditions. Specific visualizations can be specially created and practiced for specific health conditions too.

For instance, people who suffer from high blood pressure can often bring it down by vividly imaging that there are flames, like the burning wicks of candles, sticking out of their toes. This visualization will bring their energy down to their feet, thus lowering their blood pressure. They have to practice this mental imagery many times before they can master it, but once mastered it will tend to send their vital energy down to their toes and thus lower their blood pressure. Of course, chiropractic adjustments and nutritional supplements that doctors don't recommend because of ignorance can often cure the problem for good.

Another visualization specific to lowering blood pressure is to sit in a meditation posture and imagine that your head pops off your neck, is turned upside down and then rests in your lap while being held by your hands. This also moves the vital energies downward as well, which also tends to lower your blood pressure.

Cancer patients can practice imagining that their bones become a mass of blazing fire that burns off all their flesh, and next the bones themselves, which then blow away to leave a peaceful scene of empty space. Many other cancer visualizations are possible, and they take either (1) the road of activating all your vital energy (like this one) and then resting in mental peace afterwards (which is compared to a mind being like empty space) or (2) the road of attacking disease through visualizations that symbolize the body actively fighting the disease. Both roads try to activate your internal vital energy.

Representing the first road of practice, Australian psychologist **Ainslie Meares** tried a number of different visualization practices for helping cancer patients and found that the best ones were totally image free. In *Cancer and Natural Medicine*, John Boik reported Meares' finding that the most effective form of healing meditation for cancer patients was intensive sessions of imageless meditation – trying to cultivate a mind empty, like space, that witnesses everything that exists but doesn't attach to anything.

Meares found that meditation definitely reduced the anxiety, depression and pain of cancer patients, inhibited the growth of tumors in 10% of the cases ("spontaneous remissions" came in at the 10% mark due to emptiness meditation), improved the quality of life in 50% of cases, and produced significantly longer survival rates while facilitating death with dignity in 90% of the cases.

Representing the second road of practice, psychologist **Jeanne Achterberg**, author of *Imagery in Healing*, used active visualization to heal herself of a rare form of eye cancer. Afterwards she studied a group of cancer patients who were using visualization in their own battles to fight illness. Simply by examining the style and type of visualizations they used, such as the intensity of their imagery, she was able to predict with 93% accuracy which patients would completely recover and which ones would worsen or die.

Her conclusion was that cancer *survivors* had a greater ability to visualize vividly (they were able to use powerful imagery and symbols) and could hold a clear visual intention imagining themselves overpowering the cancer and their medical treatment as effective. This ties into the common observation that cancer survivors most often tend to be people who demonstrate a strong will to live and fight to survive rather than individuals who just passively give themselves over to their doctors and expect them to heal them. In order to live, you must generate a *strong will* to live and must take active steps in that direction. Visualization practice can help with that effort.

The number of authors who have therefore recommended visualizations for healing purposes include O. Carl Simonton in *Getting Well Again*, Dr. Martin Rossman in *Healing Yourself*, Rossman in *Guided Imagery for Self-Healing*, Dr. Herbert Benson in *The Relaxation Response*, and Gerald Epstein in *Healing Visualizations* among others.

For instance, Epstein once conducted a study on using mental imagery for asthma and found out that 47% of asthma sufferers who used mental imagery as a treatment were able to reduce or eliminate their medication.

On the other hand, in a control group whose members did not use mental imagery, none were able to discontinue their medication and only 19% were able to reduce it.

After extensively studying the use of visualization for healing over many years Epstein has concluded that mental imagery can definitely play a large positive role in healing and it works in a matter of minutes when used over the course of a number of days. It may not work the first few times you use it, but practiced with consistency it will start to have beneficial effects.

REGAIN MUSCLE STRENGTH

Another benefit from visualization practice is its almost inexplicable power to increase the strength of your muscles. As we saw with sports visualization practice, people who mentally rehearse the movements of muscles can actually increase their strength by nearly half the amount you would normally gain through actual exercise. Just by imagining muscle movements people are able to produce strength gains in their muscular tissues!

These conclusions were arrived at from several studies, including the previously reported experiment where researchers set out to determine strength gains in the little finger abductor muscles of healthy subjects. In this twelve-week experiment, one group of healthy volunteers was trained to just perform just "mental contractions" of little finger abduction, another performed training of physical finger abductions, and a third group served as a control group.

At the end of the twelve weeks of training, the control group showed no significant strength changes for finger abduction just as you would expect. The physical training group increased their finger abduction strength by 53%, and the finger abduction visualization group members increased their finger abduction strength by 35% - just by using their imagination!

Brian C. Clark and colleagues performed a similar study where they set out to measure changes in wrist flexor strength in three groups of healthy adults. They wanted to determine what strength gains could be achieved through mental training alone (without performing physical exercises) in the little finger abductor muscle as well as in the elbow flexor muscles.

In this experiment, for four weeks twenty-nine subjects wore a rigid cast that extended from just below the elbow to past the fingers, thus effectively immobilizing the hand and wrist. Fifteen subjects who did not wear casts served as a control group.

Half of the group with wrist-hand immobilization were asked to regularly perform a visualization exercise while the second half performed no visualization exercises at all. Those who performed visualizations were verbally guided through the imagery exercise by instructions to imagine that they were intensely contracting their wrist for five seconds and then resting for five seconds.

Just as one might expect, at the end of the four-week experiment, the two groups who wore casts had lost strength in their immobilized limbs. However, the group that performed mental visualization exercises lost 50% less strength than the non-visualizer group. In other words, the visualizers retained a lot of their strength simply due to their visualization practice!

Another advantage to having performed the visualizations while immobilized is that the nervous system's ability to fully activate the muscle (called "voluntary activation") rebounded more quickly in the visualization group compared to the group that didn't practice mental imaging.

These studies suggest that if you are immobilized for any reason whatsoever, visualization practice can help you retain your muscle strength. Even with paralysis, consistent visualization practice offers the hope of partial recovery for some of the losses in limb function. (Most doctors don't know that the Purest Colloids brand of colloidal platinum and HCG [human chorionic gonadotrophin] can help regenerate nerves to cure some types of paralysis, so visualization is a good proxy for an attempt to restore some lost function.)

SPEEDING SURGICAL RECOVERY

Visualization practice can also help you shorten rehabilitation times and recover faster after surgery. The December 2012 issue of the *Scandinavian Journal of Medicine and Science in Sports* reported a study where people who had undergone knee surgery were randomly assigned to one of two groups. Both groups received standard rehabilitation for six months after surgery, but the participants in one group also practiced guided imagery while recovering. Their visualization practice included mentally rehearsing physical therapy exercises and visualizing the physiological healing process specific to their surgery, such as scar tissue becoming flexible with gentle stretching. According to the published results, the group that practiced mental imagery showed greater improvements in knee stability and reduced levels of stress hormones.

Another experiment, published in the February 2012 issue of *Brain, Behavior, and Immunity*, focused on patients who were to have gallbladder removal. The patients were randomly assigned to either a group receiving only standard care or to one that also practiced relaxation and guided imagery for three days before and seven days after surgery. The first set of these visualization exercises focused on being relaxed and ready for surgery, and the post-surgical visualization imagery concentrated on the body's healing process. For example, participants visually imagined oxygen and nutrients traveling to the surgical wound to help the body knit the skin back together, ease discomfort and bring about soothing relief.

Compared with the group receiving only standard care, the wounds of the participants who practiced visualization imagery showed signs of faster healing and greater collagen deposition. These individuals also reported a larger reduction in stress than those who simply received standard care. Although it is not possible to determine how much of the effects were due to the visualization practice versus simply being relaxed, researchers said both factors probably worked together and that the imagery most likely enhanced the stress-reducing effects of the relaxation.

RELAXATION & PAIN MANAGEMENT

Visualization practice, such as guided imagery, can be practiced by itself, but it is frequently paired with physical relaxation techniques such as listening to music, massage, and progressive muscle relaxation. When guided imagery is paired with physical relaxation techniques, such as the wonderful *Yoga Nidra* (Swami Satyananda Saraswati), the aim is to associate the progressive sensations of relaxation with a peaceful mental image. In this way, future practice sessions involving imagery alone will recall the physical sensations of relaxation.

When our muscles get tense, pain often increases. One way to reduce pain is therefore to become more relaxed, and you can use visualization practice to help you do this. Some of the visualizations you might use along these lines are to imagine your muscles getting massaged and feeling relaxed; seeing your muscle fibers separating and loosening; feeling a warm glow within your muscles; imagining any aching part of your body feeling warm or cool and turning a soothing bluish color; imagining the redness/swelling/soreness of your body draining out of the afflicted region; imagining pain flowing out of the injured body part; feeling a numbing coolness of the sore body part; imagining "pain bubbles" leaving your body with each breath or heart beat, and so on. You will find many such visualizations in Rossman's and Epstein's books such as *Guided Imagery for Self-Healing* and *Healing Visualizations*.

Yet another strategy to distract yourself from pain is to focus on relaxing images of pleasure such as being at the beach, walking in the woods, bathing in sunshine. All these visualizations can be easily learned, but as Epstein advised they must be consistently practiced to be effective.

BRINGING QI INTO THE EQUATION

Wherever you focus your consciousness on a part of your body, your thoughts bring your vital energies to that area or simply stimulate the energies in that area via thought power because your consciousness and your Qi (internal life force or vital energy) are connected. This is why visualization can be used for sports training as well as healing. If you think of your arm and try to feel it, you will energize the Qi in that area due to the mind-body connection between thought and your internal energy. That energy or Qi, when concentrated in one area, will open up the Qi channels in the surrounding region. Since Qi is life force, this produces faster healing. You can use your will to guide your life force and produce any particular physical results you want if you simply practice hard enough and long enough.

What are the most efficient ways to practice visualization so that it brings the most Qi life force to a region of your body? There are several approaches possible as detailed in my books *Look Younger, Live Longer* and *Nyasa Yoga*.

The first approach involves *whole body visualization* techniques such as the white skeleton visualization, Mahavira's visualization of Jainism, or the Soma cream duck egg visualization. These methods activate the Qi throughout your entire body and make it available for physical and spiritual transformation, such as for healing.

The second standard approach is Nyasa practice where you concentrate on separate component pieces of the body instead of the entire body as a single whole. You bring your attention to each part of the body in turn and using visualization, imagine that each section changes its color, shines with light, feels comfortable (or excited when necessary), or feels energized. Many other methods can be used that might activate the Qi in the body part being concentrated upon. According to eastern medical traditions, when Qi eventually comes to that area, the vital energy opens up energy channels that form the scaffolding substrate of the physical body and by opening up these energy pathways it brings healing.

Yet another healing approach is to visualize processes that mimic the biochemistry of healing, such as visualizing white blood cells attacking a tumor in hopes that the mind-body connection somehow provokes a similar stimulus that produces healing. While this is a productive use of your time, it is not the best and highest visualization method. The best means is to use visualization to actively excite the Qi of your entire body, and then let go of the energy as it tries to find its own harmonious balance. If your body feels like its internal energy is comfortable, smooth and balanced, this is because your Qi flow has become smooth and regular after excitation stirred it up, and this smoothness is in turn due to more Qi channels becoming opened.

A final approach is to visualize that your body becomes one with a famous spiritual great (Buddha, Jesus, Padmasambhava, etc.) or recognized spiritual master in order that you receive the beneficial healing energies of that individual. In various Esoteric schools one actually practices projecting oneself into other people in order to transform their Qi and channels, and thus bring about their healing. One first attains this ability by training to unify their own energy or spirit with an accomplished yogic master who thereby opens your Qi channels so you can thereafter do this for others.

Yes, you can use your mind to heal your body. However, technically speaking your mind isn't what heals your body because it is your Qi – your vital energy or life force - that heals your body. With practice, your mind can learn how to activate or energize your Qi by stirring it up, and with training can begin to direct it to wherever you concentrate your thoughts. This is how you can use visualization to effect healing.

Chapter 7
HELPFUL BREATHING PRACTICES

The pursuit of excellence in sports, the desire for stronger concentration skills and the quest to become healthier can all be helped via visualization practices since they train your mental process, which in turn can affect your body's energies.

How can you then support the develop of strong visualization skills? The answer is by addressing other parts of your physical body that affect the flow of energy within it since energy flow is connected to mental fluctuations.

Let me explain …

For the best results in visualization you need to develop a steady mind. A steady mind requires that the energy flows throughout your body must be harmonious since internal energy affects your thought processes. Harmonious energy flow can easily lead to states of concentration, whereas unsettled energetic states usually inhibit concentration efforts. Therefore, to produce better internal energy flow, and thus better mental states, you need to address your body.

For more harmonious mental states, the first part of your physical body to address is your skeletal alignment. Your skeletal structure affects your posture, carriage, gait and your movement in the world. It also affects your internal energy flows. Chiropractic adjustments are a useful tool to ensure the proper alignment of your skeletal structure that will lead to better energy flow, and also provides a strong foundation for the second key physical element in improving internal energy flows: breathing practices.

Your breathing or respiration – whether coarse or smooth, long or short, shallow or deep – always affects the way your body's internal energies move. Those energies in turn affect your thoughts, and a predominance of wandering or meandering thoughts in the mind will create a jumpy mind that has trouble concentrating and forming stable mental images. Breath control can be used to pump you up or calm you down, and mental calming and concentration are required for the best visualization results.

In order to harmonize your breathing, the best type of practices are typically Chinese or Indian pranayama techniques such as taught in the *Hatha Yoga Pradipika*. In particular, the breath retention practices called kumbhaka pranayama are the ones that can help you to cultivate your internal energies and open up your energy channels. They are an aid to concentration and help produce excellent health. Proper types of breathing practices can even eradicate disease and extend your lifespan.

What you should be interested in here are breathing practices to smoothen your vital energy so that your mind becomes more peaceful and has an easier time holding the mental imagery of visualization practice. A mind that can concentrate will be able to accomplish that much more in the fields of visual thinking, inventing, mathematics, business or sports excellence.

The *Hatha Yoga Pradipika* of Indian Yoga contains many pranayama techniques and recommends that pranayama breathing exercises be practiced daily to drive impurities out of the body and regulate your internal energies. One of the most popular techniques is alternate nostril breathing where you breath in one side of the nose, hold your breath for a certain amount of time and then release the air from your lungs. By doing this for both nostrils on a rhythmical basis you harmonize both your respiration and the internal energy of your body since it is linked to your breath. When your internal energy, or Qi, has become harmonized, your mind becomes settled and it becomes easier to succeed at visualization efforts. That state of harmonious internal energy you produce is good for your health too.

Basically, the best way to create harmonious internal energy flow throughout your body is to straighten your skeletal structure through chiropractic adjustments, exercise to strengthen your heart and muscles, and perform daily pranayama breathing practices. Together your skeletal alignment, breathing, heart rate and blood pressure influence both your internal energy and mind. Pranayama will be especially helpful in making your breathing more efficient and cultivating the internal energy within your body. It will not just affect your brain and mental processes, but help to open up the energy pathways in all your tissues.

The most useful pranayama technique I know is called "9-Bottled Wind Pranayama." It is a kumbhaka pranayama (breath retention) technique that involves holding your breath nine consecutive times. Its purpose is to increase your lung capacity, make your respiratory processes more efficient, help open up your body's energy channels and improve the energy circulation within your body. This will help with healing, athletic coordination, and the ability to concentrate for long periods of time.

The 9-bottled wind practice involves *slowly* drawing air into your lungs using an alternate nostril technique, fully filling your lungs as *deeply* as possible with that air, holding the air inside for as *long* as possible while staying relaxed (not tensing any muscles but keeping them as relaxed as possible), and quickly expelling the air as *fast* as possible when you can hold it no longer.

To obtain the beneficial boosting effects to health, mental concentration or athletic performance you should start practicing the 9-bottled wind pranayama on a daily basis. If you cannot do nine full breath retentions then three is sufficient as long as each day you try to hold your breath for a longer amount of time than the previous day.

The 9-bottled wind pranayama practice steps (from my book *Look Younger, Live Longer*) are as follows:

9-Bottled Wind Pranayama Steps

(1) Sit in an upright position.

(2) Visualize your body becoming as clear as crystal.

(3) Close your mouth and also close your left nostril completely by pressing your left hand's index finger against the left nostril to shut it.

(4) Start slowly inhaling air deeply into your lungs through your right nostril. The inhalation should consist of a long breath that goes inside you and penetrates as deep into your abdomen as possible. During your inhalation, visually imagine that your body becomes filled with a shining bright light that eliminates any internal poisons or obstructions. Continue inhaling as slowly and deeply as possible until you are full and can inhale no longer.

(5) Now relax your body as much as possible while holding your breath trapped within. Hold your breath for as long as possible, but use as few muscles as possible to do so. Don't tighten any muscles, so that your Qi can start opening up all the tiny energy pathways in your body without having to fight muscle tension.

(6) When you can hold your breath no longer, exhale it as quickly and forcefully as possible through the open right nostril. Forcefully expel the air out of your body quickly to complete one cycle or round of this exercise.

(7) Repeat this exercise of slow inhalation, long retention, and forceful exhalation two more times for a total of three times for the right nostril. All the while the left nostril is kept closed while the active nostril is the right nostril.

(8) Now switch hands so that the right hand's index finger now pinches shut the right nostril while the left remains open. Inhale through your left nostril following the same instructions as before, hold your breath for as

long as possible and then forcefully exhale. Repeat this exercise three times for this side of the body. Thus, six repetitions of this exercise will now have been completed.

(9) When the left and right nostril breathings are both done, extend both your arms down to push on your lap, locking your elbows, and lift up your chest. Inhale slowly through both open nostrils, hold your breath within for as long as possible. Then exhale quickly by shooting the air out from your nostrils. Do this for a total of three times.

Altogether nine inhalations and breath retentions are performed using this simple technique of deep breath retention, which gives rise to the name of 9-step bottled wind practice.

Many people get tired of practicing this technique because it is difficult, but that is also why it is most effective. Many pranayama experts who have studied countless techniques have told me it is the most powerful of the many breathing practices they have tried. Three individuals have even told me that their lung capacity was measured by doctors and had increased by 20% after practicing this technique, which helps with asthma and other lung conditions. If it is simply reduced to using alternate nostrils to inhale air and hold your breath for as long as possible until you must forcefully exhale, and doing this as many times as possible during a short pranayama session per day, you will still get most of the benefits.

Indian Yogis who practice pranayama to live longer will perform many breath retention sessions like this throughout the day, each day trying to beat their previous best breath retention record. The world's record for breath retention is 22 minutes held by Stig Severinsen, but you don't have to train to hold your breath that long. Initially you might find it hard to hold your breath for more than 30-40 seconds, but within two weeks you can usually reach the 90-second mark. In less than a month most people can learn how to hold their breath for three minutes or longer, (especially if they combine this technique with the breath retention methods taught for freediving in the ocean that you can readily find on the internet). In this way they gradually expand their lung capacity and open up the vital energy pathways within their body. This not only lays a strong foundation for good health and longevity but also for increased mental powers after the energy channels within the brain start to open.

Another method for cultivating your internal energy so that it becomes smooth is the Soma Cream or Duck Egg visualization from Japan. It is an inner energy (nei-gong or internal breath work) exercise that mountain Master Hakuyu taught young Zen master Hakuin to help him harmonize all the vital energy within his body. Hakuin had become sick due to unbalanced internal energies and the Soma Cream visualization restored him to perfect health. The full instructions can be found in *Wild Ivy: The Spiritual Autobiography of Zen Master Hakuin* by Norman Waddell (Shambhala

Publications, 1999).

Master Hakuyu lived to an advanced age and attributed his great health and longevity to this method. At age eighty Master Hakuin was still strong and vigorous in both his body and mind, and also attributed this result to Master Hakuyu's teachings on using this visualization method. The visualization technique is as follows:

Soma Cream – Duck Egg Visualization

Imagine that a lump of soft butter the size and shape of a duck egg is placed squarely on the top of your head. As it begins to slowly melt imagine it imparting an exquisite sensation, moistening and saturating your head within and without. Imagine that as it melts and fills your body with rich fragrance it continues to ooze down, moistening your shoulders, arms, hands and chest; it permeates your heart, lungs, diaphragm, liver, stomach, trunk and intestines; moving down the spine it moistens and rejuvenates your hips, pelvis, and buttocks and then passes on through your legs, enlivening them, and eventually fills the bottom of your feet.

Imagine that this fragrant liquid, which you can visualize with a golden color or in any other auspicious manner, dissolves all the congestions that have accumulated within your organs and viscera, and it eliminates all the aches and pains and restrictions in any affected parts of your body. Imagine it flowing freely into all the areas of your body. If you like, you can practice linking the rhythm of your breathing or heart beat to the visualized flow of this soothing energy as it penetrates everywhere, which is a very good type of visualization effort, especially if you keep up this practice for years. Doing so will have untold benefits.

As the energy sinks downward into the lower body you might imagine hearing the sound of water trickling down from a higher to a lower place if that is helpful to your visualization efforts. Imagine that the soothing energy, warm and fragrant, moves down through the lower body, suffusing your legs with beneficial warmth, until it reaches the soles of the feet, where it stops.

Once you have completed the visualization, repeat it once again. Imagine the vital energy flowing downward throughout your body, gradually filling the trunk and lower regions (including your arms and legs) and suffusing everything with penetrating warmth. Imagine the final end result is that you feel as if you are sitting up to your navel in a comfortable warm bath filled with a decoction of fragrant medicinal herbs that have been assembled by a skilled physician. Imagine that the warmness you feel in your lower abdomen heals everything that might be wrong with your body or energy.

Because all things are created by the mind, this visualization will help your body reach a state of internal peace and harmony due to its ability to harmonize your internal energies. Master Hakuyu explained that with practice you will begin to feel better and enjoy greater health than you did as a youth. As your internal energy becomes more balanced, your mind will also become stronger and more stable. Your ability to concentrate and visualize will improve and you should expect improvements in other mental factors as well.

If you continue to diligently practice this visualization, it can help you calm your mind, cure illness, become better at athletic sports and other activities involving mind-body coordination, and even help with spiritual practice. Whether the results appear swiftly or slowly depends only upon how meticulously and carefully you apply yourself. For health reasons alone you should practice this visualization with total and single-minded determination because it is indisputable that the visualization of healing energy (Qi or prana) flowing through your body can help heal the body. It can even produce spiritual results.

There are many other types of kumbhaka (breath retention) pranayama techniques and nei-gong internal energy practices that can also help with concentration efforts. You can find more in my book *Nyasa Yoga* or *Internal Martial Arts Nei-gong*.

Chapter 8
SPIRITUAL VISUALIZATIONS

Across the world, visualization practice is used in Christianity, Judaism, Hinduism, Buddhism, Taoism and many other eastern religions. It is taught to spiritual aspirants because it is a way to develop a steady mind that is free (empty) of meandering thoughts. You typically call this mental state "concentration," which means that your mind is free of scattered thoughts, focused and settled on one particular topic.

We have already covered the solid scientific findings which tell us that visualization efforts, mental rehearsal or mental imagery practice can create new neural pathways in the brain and even change its structure. However, while this is incredibly important, eastern religions focus on an entirely different physical aspect of the practice other than this.

The eastern spiritual schools – such as Yoga, Hinduism, Buddhism and Taoism - explain that our body has Qi channels or energy pathways that pass through every muscle fiber and cell. These are like the energetic scaffolding of atomic bonds between all the atoms in the body. These are the energy routes through which our life force (Qi) flows. If you clear these pathways of blockages then your body will get warmer, your muscles will soften, you will become more flexible, joyful and healthier and establish the foundation for a longer life. If you are an athlete and open up these channels, your energy will flow much better, you will become able to achieve higher states of mind-body coordination and it will become easier to achieve states of peak performance. You can only achieve the state of "flow" in sports if you have cultivated your Qi and opened your Qi channels, and visualization practice is one of the methods that helps you do so.

When you practice concentration exercises, such as visualization, the act of mental focusing quiets your mind. When your mind quits, then your true vitality (life force, kundalini, or Yang Qi) begins to stir and progress through all your body's Qi channels. This result is only helpful and never harmful even though it often produces unusual symptoms.

If your Qi channels start opening due to the result of concentration practices like visualization, the normal sequence of progress is that your mind starts to become clearer. With greater clarity and focus you can then more accurately observe your thoughts. Because you are now more self-aware of your activities and what is going on within your mind, you make better decisions that will change your life in a positive way.

Through visualization practice, whose proficiency you can build by practicing previous exercises, you can learn how to steadily hold a complicated image in your mind while ignoring all the other meandering thoughts that randomly arise and then flicker away. By concentrating on trying to create a stable mental visual image, you will learn how to ignore random thoughts other than that image.

After you can finally form a stable image in your mind and hold it for some time you should then let go of the imagery that you built through focused concentration. Since it takes concentration effort to hold an image, when you finally let go of it your mind will feel free and at ease, like an ox who feels happy when the heavy collar around his neck is finally dropped off after a day of hard plowing.

At that time, the fact that your mind is now relaxed and empty of effort will allow your Qi to arise within your body. Free of any attachments to thought since you have just abandoned them, it will then be free to begin working its way through your Qi channels to open them. This is the purpose of all preliminary stage spiritual practices. You practice some form of concentration – in this case holding visual images steady in your mind – in order to tie up your thoughts (thus abandoning any focus on body sensations you might try to guide through thoughts) so that once free of attachments your Qi will become activated and arise.

Aside from the fact that visualization exercises to form steady mental images without becoming distracted teaches you how to concentrate (ignore wandering thoughts), are there any other benefits besides developing concentration skills?

BENEFITS OF VISUALIZATION PRACTICE

The first benefit, of course, is the progressive development of visual thinking skills, which we saw has helped countless scientists, mathematicians and inventors. Visualization practice can train you to be able to think visually. It enables you to develop visual thinking skills if you pursue this route of training.

Business people can also use visualization practice to help them change their habits and behaviors, achieve goals, rehearse performances and become the people they want to be.

Athletes can and do regularly use it to perfect their skills, summon confidence during games, and to help win athletic competitions. They use it in the pursuit of peak sports performance.

Sick people can use visualization skills to stimulate their life force and help heal themselves. Basically, visualization practice can help us cure our body of disease by igniting its vital energy.

A biological fact is that your Qi and consciousness are linked. With just a little bit of effort you can easily prove that the vital energy within your body can be moved by your thoughts – your Qi will go to wherever you place your concentration - so eastern religions state that your Qi rides on (follows) your thoughts.

When your Qi arrives in any body region due to focusing on that area with visualization (or some other form of concentration), the Qi will begin to open up the channels in that vicinity. In opening Qi channels, you can banish latent illness and lay the foundations for increased health and longevity.

All spiritual practice depends upon building a foundation of health. Spiritual practice also depends upon the fact that your Qi and consciousness are linked; your energy within your body can be moved by your thoughts. Wherever your concentration goes in your body, your Qi will also go there. Those energies will then mass at that point to open up the Qi channels in the vicinity, which will make your body healthier (and improve sports skills) since your energy flow will be much more efficient.

KASINA CONCENTRATION PRACTICE

We previously encountered kasina visualization practice, which is a special type of concentration practice that uses colored shapes. Kasina meditation has been used in India for thousands of years. The 5th-century Indian Buddhist monk Buddhaghosa describes kasina visualization practice in the *Visuddhimagga* ("Path of Purification") and it can also be found in the Buddhist monk Asanga's *Yogacarabhumi sastra* (in the *Samāhitabhūmi* section).

Kasina visualization practice is actually a form of visual concentration practice that has no religious affiliation with any school or tradition. It is just a technique of mental exercise you can use to build up your concentration skills, visualization skills and visual thinking skills.

There are traditionally forty different types of kasina concentration objects, which is a large enough selection that one or more will appeal to the different temperaments of people seeking to use it. The number and types of concentration objects listed are just indicative of what you can try once you understand the technique. If you apply the principles of logic and common sense, you can use many different types of objects for visualization practice. You can even invent new ones that might be especially useful for sports or health purposes.

The basic kasina practice involves concentrating on certain colors, elements, shapes or meditations, holding them in your mind, and thereby learn how to develop a stable mind. You can also do this with an emotion, but for our purposes we will only discuss the kasina objects that can be used in visualization practice.

Whenever you can hold an image in your mind without distraction the resulting mental stability is called a concentration or stable mind. With kasina visualization practice you can gradually gain proficiency at generating a stable mind by holding onto a visual image for as long as possible. When you can hold onto the image without losing concentration you will then have achieved one of the objectives of the practice.

The most common type of kasina visualization is to visualize a disk of a specific color that you place against a wall several feet in front of you. When you sit on the floor in a meditation posture and face the wall the disk should be in front of you at eye level.

The traditional kasina instructions suggest that you practice visualizing the colors blue, green, yellow, red and white. However, you should also add orange, purple, black, copper (brown), silver and gold to this basic list. Actually, you can and should practice visualizing *all the different colors of the rainbow* one by one, but let's pretend you just want to practice by visualizing the color yellow, which tends to lighten one's mood.

To do so you would buy yellow construction paper, cut out a large yellow circle, and then tape it to the wall at eye level height in front of you, several feet away. When you sit in a meditation posture you want to be able to open your eyes and see the disk clearly so that you can practice the yellow color visualization. Sitting several feet from the wall, you should look at the colored disk for a while, close your eyes and then try to visualize it within your mind.

The traditional instructions in the *Visuddhimagga* are to use a circle made of colored earth, but you don't have to restrict yourself to a circle of earth as it suggests. You can and *should* try visualizing different shapes in different colors such as squares, triangles, stars, crescents, half circles, rectangles and so on. You will find that the most important colors to use are auspicious colors that raise your energy such as yellow, red, gold and silver.

For someone just starting out, practice visualizing (1) a yellow square, (2) blue circle and, (3) red triangle and then progress onwards from there. You can also turn these into 3D shapes.

Once again, you want to become able *to visualize all the different colors of the rainbow* – red, orange, yellow, green, blue, indigo and violet as well as white, black, copper (brown), silver and gold. Gold, silver, white, yellow, orange and red are very important for raising your energy. Green, blue and black are useful for lowering excessive energy.

These colors can also be useful in other visualization practices, especially the advanced visualization practices used in the spiritual schools. Vajrayana Buddhists, for instance, practice visualizing complicated mandalas and elaborate pictures of Buddhas that contain many different colors and shapes. Navajo Indians create colorful sandpaintings that are similar to Buddhist mandalas and can be used for mental practice. Hindus practice visualizing Yantras as well as colorful images of various deities who represent cosmic forces. Kashmir Shaivists (and members of various Yoga schools) visualize images of "chakras" within their body.

The Jewish school of Merkabah mysticism also uses visualization practices as does Christianity. *Spiritual Exercises*, written by the 16th century Spaniard St. Ignatius of Loyola, had a tremendous impact teaching Jesuit priests and Christian monks to practice visualizing certain scenes of Christ's life (such as the Nativity, Passion, Crucifixion, Resurrection and Ascension). It is said to have brought about profound inner changes in individuals, and its influence over 400 years has been described as "incalculable."

These are just a few examples proving that visualization exercises are a spiritual practice used in many religions! The reason is because visualization helps you calm your mind, learn concentration skills, and can open up your energy pathways. When your Qi channels open and your vitality flows, this is what prepares people for advanced spiritual experiences. Hence, this is why people concentrate on internally visualizing pictures of chakras and deities. When you project such images inside your body, it can also serve as a technique to bring Qi to internal body regions so that the Qi channels open and one becomes more fit for the spiritual path.

Visualization practice itself does not open chakras at all, nor does it turn you into a deity. It simply gets rid of wandering thoughts so that your Qi can freely arise without too many thought attachments; your Qi cannot flow freely if your mind is always following meandering thoughts that are connected to your Qi. After your Qi arises and clears open your Qi channels then you can begin to cultivate more advanced states of mental refinement and clarity. These advanced mental states, or states of higher concentration, are always clear states of mind absent of meandering thoughts. Your Qi follows your thoughts because of the mind-body connection of vital energy and consciousness, so only when thought is silenced via concentration can your real Qi be released from its normal connection to thoughts and start opening up the Qi channels within you.

The *Visuddhimagga* does not just recommend visualization practice on colors but visualization of the earth, water, fire, air and space elements too.

You can practice visualizing that your entire body becomes one of these elements, or that you see the image of your element in your mind while feeling its texture within your body. There are many other ways you can practice these visualizations.

Different colors and sensory feelings can be associated with these elements when they are being visualized. When visualizing that your body becomes fire, for instance, you typically imagine that it becomes flaming luminescent red in color and that you feel the energy pulsing all over inside you. However, you can also imagine a feeling of heat or surging energy everywhere within you in conjunction with a feeling of joy, elation or exhilaration. Whenever you perform spiritual practices and wish to open up Qi channels, you can try to simultaneously evoke the feelings of elation, joy, exhilaration or ecstasy at the same time since this will help stir up your vital energy and raise your Yang Qi. Perform visualizations both with and without this extra emotional content.

When you feel your energy moving as a result of this type of practice, then you are succeeding. People sometimes get scared when their internal energy starts to move due to kasina practice, but that movement is a major purpose of the practice.

When imaging that your body becomes the water element you can imagine that it becomes blue (or white like milk) all over and the energetic feeling inside is sloshy and *cooling* like water. You can also add an emotional component to the experience that you would normally associate with soothing water. If you were to imagine that your body became pure moonlight, you would also imagine that it was pure, cool and peaceful like the moon.

The basic geometric shapes to master in visualization practice are the circle, square and triangle followed by the oval, ellipse, crescent, rectangle, trapezoid, pentagon, and hexagon. If you are motivated and have learned how to visualize these basic flat shapes, you can try to visualize a heptagon, octagon, nonagon, and decagon.

After gaining proficiency at visualizing these geometric figures and then being able to hold them steady in your mind, you can next try to mentally move the images about, twisting and rotating them, making them larger or smaller, changing their colors or putting them inside one another. An even higher skill level is learning how to project them onto the environment by superimposing their image on whatever you are looking at. You can train your mind to do this just as it can be trained to handle many different types of simultaneously independent activity, but most people never choose to undertake such difficult training.

Another skill is to turn the flat images into 3D shapes such as spheres, half-spheres, cylinders, discs or doughnuts made from a circle; eggs made from ellipses; cubes or rectangular solids (boxes) made from a square; or pyramids, wedges, prisms and cones made from a triangle. Basically, you can practice visualizing the Platonic solids and how they are formed. Afterwards you should practice gaining proficiency in manipulating them.

To test your skills at manipulating images, try unfolding the solids to discover their shape as a flat surface cutout, such as unfolding a square to make a cross. Once you can mentally unfold a geometrical shape, practice marking one side a certain color, refolding the pattern into the shape, and rotating the solid to see where the image will land. This exercise develops your "**spatial reasoning**" skills (the ability to manipulate, rotate, or change the position of an object in your mind) and you can practice these skills with tests readily available on the internet. Spatial reasoning or spatial intelligence, which can be increased by developing your visualization skills, is useful in many technical fields such as engineering, architecture, mathematics, astronomy and chemistry. Developing these skills – because they also require you to build concentration skills - is also a type of spiritual practice!

One of the reasons I personally began visualization practice is because I wanted to increase my spatial reasoning and spatial visualization skills. With time and practice these skills definitely get better, but it takes hard, consistent effort.

Studies have shown that men and women initially differ in their spatial reasoning skills but after 21 days of daily practice the differences can start to disappear. Using Google SketchUp, which is a free 3D dynamic sketching software, people can easily work on building these skills.

You can next practice visualizing real objects such as a pair of dice (based on cubes), Christmas ornaments (made from a sphere), a candle (made from a cylinder), ice cream cone (made from a triangle turned into a cone), or soccer ball (a truncated icosahedron, which is one of the Archimedean solids). All sorts of real world images can be imagined and manipulated once you develop the basic visualization powers and learn how to manipulate mental forms.

Once you have mastered basic geometrical shapes, spiritual aspirants can visualize shapes within their body to activate their Qi since a focus of attention would bring Qi to that area and thus open up Qi channels in the surrounding vicinity. For instance, Christians reciting the Prayer of Jesus often visualize a flame at their heart while Buddhists who recite the Zhunti mantra visualize the image of a Buddha or circle of Buddhas in their heart. Some practitioners visualize a shining Sanskrit or Hebrew letter at the heart. Yogis cultivating kundalini often visualize a red triangle in their lower abdomen or at the base of their spine. In Gnostic spiritual practice the adherents visualize a sun over their heads, which tends to open up the ascending nerve channels in the brain. Those visualizing chakras or any shining shape in the center of their body tend to open up the Qi channels in that vicinity too. These are just a few examples of how and why visualization exercises are used for spiritual practice.

CANDLE VISUALIZATION

Another basic visualization, since once mastered it can also be used as an activation mechanism inside your body for Qi arousal, is to look at a burning candle, next close your eyes, and then visualize the candle. Being able to visualize the bright flame is the most important part of this practice. After you can visualize the candle, you can place the image of the flame inside your body, which is useful in the pelvis, abdomen (solar plexus), heart, throat and brain.

This particular visualization practice is especially important because visualizing a candle flame is extremely useful in other spiritual practices involving the stimulation of Qi at points on your body. Many traditions that use visualization exercises stress flames and fires for this reason since those images can be used to stimulate your Qi.

As explained in *Twenty-five Doors to Meditation*, there are many concentration practices based on focusing your vision on an object. If you master the basic technique of concentrating upon and observing an object then you open the door to hundreds of possible practices. To achieve this mastery, it is once again best to start with a candle. To practice, you place it about three to five feet in front of you, and simply become mentally absorbed in focusing on it while ignoring any other meandering thoughts that pop into your mind. Besides a candle, the best objects to are those joyful or auspicious in tone like a crystal, bright light, or inspiring/happy religious statue or picture.

To train your powers of concentration you focus on an object while ignoring all other wandering thoughts that arise in your mind, and eventually they will drop away. With practice you can train to close your eyes and become so focused on your mentally created object that you can make it smaller and smaller in your mind. You can only do this if the intensity of your concentration increases, and this requires training. In some Yoga schools they ask aspirants to mentally visualize the counting of thousands of drops, or tiny spheres rotating inside other spheres, and all sorts of other concentration challenges.

In doing this you don't try to describe the object in your mind or give rise to any type of internal dialogue. You just become absorbed in the object as the sole center of your attention. As with a mathematician trying to solve a problem, you become totally involved in a problem and focused on just that one thing. In the Zen school, the focus on an indecipherable koan serves the same function of tying up your attention.

THE WHITE SKELETON VISUALIZATION

As we have previously stated, all spiritual progress depends upon having a foundation of good health. It requires cultivating your Qi and Qi channels - the acupuncture meridians within which the Qi (vital force) in your body runs. Many practices are used throughout the world's religions to help aspirants cultivate and purify their Qi and Qi channels, in effect purifying them, and since you now know this you might be able to decipher which ones do this in your own particular spiritual tradition.

Visualizing the muscles and organs of your body, focusing on feeling them while visualizing them inside you at their proper anatomical positions, is also a type of Qi and Qi channel practice. It is a higher form of visualization exercise than concentrating on an object since it directly touches your Qi life force. This type of practice always leads to greater health, longevity and spiritual progress.

One of the most powerful of these visualization practices (which produces even greater benefits) is to visualize the bones of your body, and then later your muscles after the Qi and Qi channels within and along the bones have been "awakened" due to your practice. This visualization exercise is called the "white skeleton visualization" method. It comes from ancient India, and it is useful for health, sports training and spiritual progress.

The white skeleton visualization, which is particularly used in Buddhism, involves individually visualizing all the bones of your body as shining with a bright white light – as bright as you can possibly imagine. This energizes your Qi that flows parallel to your skeletal structure. Since your skeleton stretches throughout your entire body the invigorated energy flow due to visualization (Qi follows your thoughts) will start to open up all the Qi channels in your muscles.

Once again the principle behind this type of visualization practice is as follows. Through focused concentration and attention you can bring your vital energy to a bone – or stimulate the energy of that bone - by visualizing that it is white in color and shining with a bright light. Wherever you place your mind within your body, your Qi will move there due to the mental focus. It will mass at that point or simply become stimulated at that point. Therefore this visualization will bring Qi to the bone and its surrounding tissues (or stimulate it) and this is what opens up the Qi channels in the areas along the length of the bone that you visualize.

The white skeleton visualization can be practiced when you are sitting or lying flat on your back, though sitting in a meditation posture is best. There are many variations of the basic energizing practice so we will just discuss the basic principles. The principle is to use visualization power to energize your Qi so that it starts opening your Qi channels. Many more related details can be found in my book, *Nyasa Yoga*.

If you understand the basic principles and what you are trying to accomplish with this visualization practice then you can create all sorts of variations. It just depends upon understanding that the target is to (1) activate/stimulate your Qi in order to (2) open your Qi channels, (3) which is done by using visualizations to stimulate your Qi into moving, (4) which works since your Qi and consciousness are linked. Thus, while in sports training we use visualization to forge new neural pathways, and while inventors and scientists use it to develop skills at visual thinking, here you can use visualization images – which are thoughts - to move the energy of your body.

To practice the white skeleton visualization, you should first make yourself comfortable and take a couple of deep breaths to release any tension you feel in your body.

The White Skeleton Visualization Practice

Starting at your left big toe, begin to visualize that you no longer have flesh on the left foot and that your two left big toe bones shine with a dazzling white light. Try to imagine that the naked bones shine with as bright a light as possible.

First visualize that the two bones of your left big toe are shining as a bright white light, and then move leftwards to simultaneously visualize that all of the other toe bones on your left foot (there are three bones per toe) are shining with a bright white light.

Try to feel the bones when you do this, or the energy in the area, or heat in the area because you want to send Qi to this region. Try to *feel the energy* in the bones or surrounding them by grabbing it if you can. The more "real" or vivid you can make this visualization the better.

When you can finally visualize your toes shining with bright white light, maintain that vision of the left toe bones and switch sides to start visualizing that the bones of your right big toe are also shining with a dazzling white light. Then visualize that all of the toes of your right foot are shining brightly.

Next, visualize all of the other bones within your left foot are shining with bright white light, then all of the bones in your right foot. Now the bones of both feet should be seen in your mind as shining with a bright white light. You actually try to feel the energy within the feet as you do this because you are trying to activate the Qi in the feet to open up its many Qi channels.

Continuing, visualize your left ankle bones and then right ankle bones shining with a dazzling bright light. All the bones in your feet should now be simultaneously seen in inner vision as shining with a bright white light.

Try to feel the energy in the feet and along the bones; if the feet get warm it means that your Qi is starting to open up your Qi channels in this area.

Proceeding higher, start visualizing that your left tibia and fibula (lower-leg bones) are shining with a bright white light, and then do the same for your right lower-leg bones. Remember to visualize that all the flesh is stripped off your bones and all the exposed bones are shining with a bright white light. (An alternative is to visualize that your bones are brightly shining while within your skin and flesh.)

Gradually working your way up your body, continue visualizing that your body is just a set of shining white bones. Visualize your leg and feet bones all the way through to the bones of your pelvic girdle, and then start visualizing the bones of your spine. In time you will certainly feel warm at those areas because of the activation of your Qi due to this method.

Since this method helps you open up your Qi channels, it is great for both athletes and those wishing to cure illness to become healthier.

Once you go up through your hips and spine to reach your neck, make sure you progressively visualize the bones of both arms as well as your hands and fingers.

After visualizing the bones in your hands and fingers so that your whole lower body is done up to your neck, afterwards you end with a visualization of your skull bones also shining, together with the rest of your body, with a bright white light.

At the initial stages of this practice it is not important that you correctly visualize each individual bone of your body with extreme accuracy, though that is an excellent exercise in concentration. This is where people always go wrong. They forget that *the purpose of the practice is to activate your Qi along the extent of your entire body, using your bones as the general structural guideline for the shape of the body. Therefore, as long as you are activating your Qi along its entire structure, whether or not you can visualize your bones correctly, or be anatomically perfect, is irrelevant. You just want to activate your Qi everywhere in the body. Only at advanced stages of cultivation need you be anatomically correct.*

Activating your Qi, since it is the point of the exercise, is more important than learning how to perfectly visualize your anatomical skeleton. However, there is also a benefit to being able to actually visualize a perfect skeleton. The result of visualizing your skeleton with accuracy is good concentration skills.

"Good to great" concentration skills are one of the benefits from trying to visualize mandalas, as practiced in Vajrayana Buddhism, and Yantras as practiced in Hinduism. Visualizing a complicated Yantra or mandala has no other benefit than helping you learn concentration because the sustained focus banishes scattered thoughts from your mind.

Visualization practice requires so much concentration that your mind eventually tires, like a computer that slows down due to excessive computational demands. When you can finally hold a picture in your mind with stability then when you can no longer hold it you should release your visualization to rest in an empty mental state of peace. In that state your Qi will come up, since it always arises when the mind becomes quiet, and in that way visualization practice becomes a meditation method.

Finally, while this is primarily a mental visualization practice, it is helpful to be happy and joyful when doing this visualization (and to feel like you are offering your flesh away as a type of giving or offering) simply because these emotions will raise the Yang Qi in your body. This is why you cultivate the fervor of emotional joy and offerings on the path of religion.

When one imagines that the energy of a spiritual master unifies with their body in order to open up its Qi channels, which is a spiritual practice done in many schools that has similarities with the skeleton visualization technique, one should also think of positive thoughts during the unification practice. The purpose of this type of practice – such as visualizing you become one with the spirit of a beautified enlightened being or deity (such as Shiva, Krishna, Lakshmi, Vajrayogini, Buddha, Jesus, Thor, Zeus, Padmasambhava, Majursi, etc.) is to call upon the spiritual powers of great enlightened ones to help open up your Qi channels.

MAHAVIRA'S FIRE VISUALIZATION

Another visualization technique for cultivating the Qi of your body was introduced by Mahavira, the founder of the Jains. It is excellent for giving your body a feeling of energy inside.

For this visualization method, you imagine that there is a large lotus flower inside your body at the level of your navel. Imagine that is bright red in color, pointing upwards, and burning with red flames that shoot upwards and protrude out from the center of your head.

The reason you must visualize the flames reaching out from the top of your head is because concentrating on a point outside of your body will help draw your Qi to that point. Therefore, this visualization will help draw your Qi energies through the left and right branches of your spinal nerves that separate in the brain and reach to its top. These left and right ascending nerve bundles, although inside the brain, are symbolized as external horns in most cultural traditions since that is what they internally look like. They can only be opened by the ascending Qi in your body, which is why you visualize fire, Qi, shining light or other images to guide Qi up these nerve bundles to open them.

For the rest of this visualization exercise, you should also imagine at the level of your heart another bright red lotus flower, but this one is inverted. Visualize that the flames originating from your belly flower blaze upwards and reach the inverted heart flower, which is turned upside down, and that the flames grow intense between these two lotus flowers.

You should imagine that the flames eventually fill the trunk of your body filled with Qi, which turns flaming bright red and feels excited all over. Eventually this fiery red luminescence extends to your entire body and you should soak in that luminescence trying to feel any full-body sensations you can evoke. Try to feel the surging energy everywhere as your entire body turns into glowing red embers. Try to stimulate your energy into surging (moving) using the imagination of fire as the catalyst.

Try to also feel exhilarated, elated, happy, enthusiastic when doing this visualization because these emotions also raise your Yang Qi. This exercise is a type of cleansing of your body that uses fire instead of water.

After you visualize your entire body glowing red with energy or fire, and after you feel corresponding energy sensations within you (due to your efforts to arouse them), imagine that a strong wind blows off all the embers and then a heavy, clear rain falls from above washing all the ashes away. Imagine that the body you now have left is crystal clear, transparent and pure.

When you finally visualize this, then let go of all the imaging and rest your mind in empty space (just as you did for the white skeleton visualization). While resting with an empty mind, mentally observe (just witness) the sensations that arise within your body of internal energy from the moving energy. This feeling of energy moving inside you is *supposed to happen* and heals you by opening up your energy channels.

ENERGIZED RED BODY PRACTICE

Yet another visualization technique is to vividly imagine (once again with elated happy feelings since this activates your Yang Qi) that your body becomes luminescent red with energy, impregnated with fire, or entirely flames. Some schools suggest imagining that you become surging lava, a blazing sun, or emanating sunshine. Use whatever visualization method works to enable you to imagine that your body is the fire element and to feel stirred up energy sensations inside you. The sole purpose of this visualization effort is to stimulate and move, activate or energize your Qi.

Red fire energy is traditionally used across nearly every spiritual tradition to represent Yang Qi, or positive energy. The deep subconscious image of fire within our minds is also energizing as well.

To raise the Yang Qi energy within you, some schools teach you to visualize a fiery red triangle in your pelvis or heart region or at the base of the spine, and to hold onto that image. The concentration on a point within your body will bring more energy/Qi to the area and open up your Qi channels leading to more health and vitality.

93

FIRE CEREMONIES

Many religions, such as Zoroastrianism, Shingon, and Hinduism have fire ceremonies, but people don't know the real reason for this. In most fire ceremonies, participants are supposed to sit around a blazing fire, stare at the flames and try to feel the energy arising inside them. They are supposed to imagine that their entire body becomes fire or becomes energized like fire since this stimulates the Qi within it. Unfortunately, most people who attend these ceremonies don't know these instructions. When you feel the heat of the fire penetrate you and see the flames you should match these stimuli with efforts to arouse your internal energy and start it moving.

When your Qi is activated in this way it will start coursing through your body and all its energy meridians, especially the Qi channels in your spine. When you finally feel like there is energy all over your body due to your stimulation efforts, you should next try to diffuse it throughout your body in an evenly balanced manner and then let go of clinging to any of the sensations that arise. You should observe the sensations that arise, but you should not try to block them or cling to them. In Buddhism this is called anapana practice. You can now try to smooth out any sensations of internal energy blockage or obstruction in order to help open up other energy pathways within your body. In the long run this will bring you more health and vitality.

OPENING THE SPINE

There are many Yogic, Tantric and Upanishadic practices that use visualizations to open up the Qi channels in your body, particularly in your spine. The instructions for many of these practices can be found in Swami Niranjanananda Saraswati's excellent book, *Dharana Darhan*, which is highly recommended.

Kriya Yoga, which is special type of kundalini yoga for cultivating your Qi and channels, also uses visualizations to cultivate the Qi of your body. It focuses on removing any blockages in your spine so that your Qi can ascend upwards into the brain, which produces all the normal Qi benefits as well as helping with memory, concentration, awareness and relaxation. Since it is non-denominational, Kriya Yoga is very helpful for individuals of any religious denomination who are ardently working on a spiritual path of practice.

I recommend several excellent books on Kriya Yoga that provide descriptions of visualization exercises:

• Paramahansa Yogananda's *Kriya Yoga*

- *A Systematic Course in Ancient Tantric Techniques of Yoga and Kriya* by Swami Satyananda Saraswati
- *Kriya Yoga* by Paramahamsa Hariharananda
- *Kriya Yoga The Science of Life Force* by Swami Nityananda Giri
- *Kriya Secrets Revealed* by J.C. Stevens. This is one of the best books available on Kriya Yoga. It contains many useful exercises for opening up the spinal Qi channels along its length.

Chinese Taoism also has a number of visualization practices you can try for opening up the spinal Qi routes, which is called the microcosmic circulation.

It is impossible to duplicate all of the visualization exercises from these various books since they contain many materials; the point is to use visualization efforts, in conjunction with willpower, to move your Qi along Qi routes to help open them. My book, *Nyasa Yoga*, provides a short synopsis of the best internal Qi exercises along these lines drawn from a variety of the world's spiritual traditions.

Chapter 9
CONCLUSION

PET imaging scans of the brain, and other advanced imaging techniques, indisputably prove that the same parts of the brain are activated whether people are visually imaging something or actually experiencing it. This can be used to our benefit if we set out to master visualization practice.

Your optical cortex and the energy pathways in the occipital part of your brain are activated when you visualize an image. Your auditory cortex is activated when you imagine music, and your sensory cortex is activated when you imagine the sense of touch. Whether you do something for real or simply imagine it, your brain will create and transmit signals similar to those produced by direct experience.

You can use this connection between the visually imagined and the real for superior sports training. You can also employ visualization to move the energy within your body for healing purposes or for spiritual practice. You can use visualization practice to develop visual thinking skills, concentration skills, problem solving skills or new behaviors that you wish to master.

Visualization practice trains you to develop new mental powers that can be used in many ways, all of which can be immensely productive for your life. People of all ages can master visualization powers, but the earlier you get started at the challenge the more beneficial can be their impact. If you really think that visualization powers can be useful, I hope that you can introduce these many practices to others who might benefit.

ABOUT THE AUTHOR

William Bodri is the author of several health and self-help books including:

- *Quick, Fast, Done: Simple Time Management Secrets from Some of History's Greatest Leaders*
- *Move Forward: Powerful Strategies for Creating Better Outcomes in Life*
- *How to Create a Million Dollar Unique Selling Proposition*
- *Breakthrough Strategies of Wall Street Traders: 17 Remarkable Traders Reveal Their Top Performing Investment Strategies*
- *Super Investing: 5 Proven Methods for Beating the Market and Retiring Rich*
- *High Yield Investments, Hard Assets and Asset Protection Strategies*
- *Super Cancer Fighters*
- *Look Younger, Live Longer*
- *The Little Book of Meditation*
- *Meditation Case Studies*
- *The Little Book of Hercules*
- *Internal Martial Arts Nei-gong*
- *What is Enlightenment?*
- *Detox Cleanse Your Body Quickly and Completely*
- *Nyasa Yoga*

If you enjoyed this book you would probably enjoy his titles *Internal Martial Arts Nei-gong, Look Younger, Live Longer, The Little Book of Hercules, The Little Book of Meditation, Nyasa Yoga* and *Move Forward*, all of which contain related materials.

Made in the USA
Monee, IL
08 January 2023

24848373R00059